CAMBRIDGE LIBRARY COLLECTION

Books of enduring scholarly value

Polar Exploration

This series includes accounts, by eye-witnesses and contemporaries, of early expeditions to the Arctic and the Antarctic. Huge resources were invested in such endeavours, particularly the search for the North-West Passage, which, if successful, promised enormous strategic and commercial rewards. Cartographers and scientists travelled with many of the expeditions, and their work made important contributions to earth sciences, climatology, botany and zoology. They also brought back anthropological information about the indigenous peoples of the Arctic region and the southern fringes of the American continent. The series further includes dramatic and poignant accounts of the harsh realities of working in extreme conditions and utter isolation in bygone centuries.

Lieut. John Irving, R.N., of H.M.S. *Terror*, in Sir John Franklin's Last Expedition to the Arctic Regions

John Irving (1815–1847?) was a lieutenant on board H.M.S. *Terror* during Sir John Franklin's fateful expedition, and had the melancholy distinction of being the first identifiable body to be found by a subsequent search party – that of the U.S. officer Frederick Schwatka – in 1878. Irving was identified by a silver medal, won for mathematics in 1830. His remains were brought back to Britain and reburied in his home town, Edinburgh, and at the request of Irving's father this 'memorial sketch', including some of the young lieutenant's letters to his family, was published in 1881 by Benjamin Bell (1810–83), great-grandfather of the surgeon Joseph Bell, Conan Doyle's model for Sherlock Holmes. As well as the touching memoir, the work includes details of the various search and rescue attempts, and a reconstructed chronology by Clements Markham of the Franklin expedition up to its disastrous end.

Cambridge University Press has long been a pioneer in the reissuing of out-of-print titles from its own backlist, producing digital reprints of books that are still sought after by scholars and students but could not be reprinted economically using traditional technology. The Cambridge Library Collection extends this activity to a wider range of books which are still of importance to researchers and professionals, either for the source material they contain, or as landmarks in the history of their academic discipline.

Drawing from the world-renowned collections in the Cambridge University Library and other partner libraries, and guided by the advice of experts in each subject area, Cambridge University Press is using state-of-the-art scanning machines in its own Printing House to capture the content of each book selected for inclusion. The files are processed to give a consistently clear, crisp image, and the books finished to the high quality standard for which the Press is recognised around the world. The latest print-on-demand technology ensures that the books will remain available indefinitely, and that orders for single or multiple copies can quickly be supplied.

The Cambridge Library Collection brings back to life books of enduring scholarly value (including out-of-copyright works originally issued by other publishers) across a wide range of disciplines in the humanities and social sciences and in science and technology.

Lieut. John Irving, R.N. of H.M.S. *Terror*, in Sir John Franklin's Last Expedition to the Arctic Regions

A Memorial Sketch with Letters

BENJAMIN BELL

CAMBRIDGE
UNIVERSITY PRESS

CAMBRIDGE
UNIVERSITY PRESS

University Printing House, Cambridge, CB2 8BS, United Kingdom

Cambridge University Press is part of the University of Cambridge.

It furthers the University's mission by disseminating knowledge in the pursuit of
education, learning and research at the highest international levels of excellence.

www.cambridge.org
Information on this title: www.cambridge.org/9781108071857

© in this compilation Cambridge University Press 2014

This edition first published 1881
This digitally printed version 2014

ISBN 978-1-108-07185-7 Paperback

Memorial Sketch

OF

Lieut. John Irving, R.N

Edinburgh: Printed by Thomas and Archibald Constable,

FOR

DAVID DOUGLAS.

LONDON . . . . HAMILTON, ADAMS, AND CO.
CAMBRIDGE . . . . . . MACMILLAN AND CO.
GLASGOW . . . . JAMES MACLEHOSE.

LIEUT. JOHN IRVING, R.N.

OF H.M.S. "TERROR,"

IN SIR JOHN FRANKLIN'S LAST EXPEDITION
TO THE ARCTIC REGIONS

A Memorial Sketch with Letters

EDITED BY

BENJAMIN BELL, F.R.C.S.E.

EDINBURGH: DAVID DOUGLAS

1881

PREFATORY NOTE.

IT has occurred to a few friends of the late Lieutenant John Irving, R.N., whose remains were recently interred with Naval honours and much public sympathy, in the Dean Cemetery, Edinburgh, that a brief yet reliable memoir of the deceased might be acceptable to many of his countrymen. The circumstance that he was the only individual of Sir John Franklin's Expedition whose identity has been proved,—an Expedition the history and results of which, although in many respects successful and glorious, are still veiled in much mystery,—invests his name with a peculiar interest, and seems to justify this endeavour to draw attention to a character of rare excellence, which, unless he had thus become, in some measure, a representative man, would have been allowed to pass into oblivion without special notice.

The present Editor having been requested by Major-General Irving to undertake this office of friendship, has much satisfaction in doing his best. A series of letters from the deceased to his early friend and messmate, the present William E. Malcolm, Esq. of Burnfoot, and another series addressed to his sister-in-law, Mrs. L. H. Irving, have greatly facilitated the task. Much obligation is also felt to C. R. Markham, Esq., C.B., Secretary to the Royal Geographical Society, for several communications which will be more particularly acknowledged afterwards.

The Record discovered by Sir L. M'Clintock, introduced at p. 136, has been photographed from the original for this publication by Mr. W. Griggs, London, through the courtesy of the authorities.

EDINBURGH, *May* 1881.

CONTENTS.

———

CHAPTER I.

1815–1834.

Birth—Parentage—Colonel Lewis Hay—Mrs. Irving—At
New Academy, Edinburgh—Royal Naval College,
Portsmouth—Medal in mathematics—His brothers and
sister—Enters the Navy in 1830—The "Cordelia"—
The "Belvidera"—Mr. W. E. Malcolm, Mr. George
Kingston, his shipmates, ... 1

CHAPTER II.

1834–1837.

Correspondence with W. E. Malcolm—Idea of leaving
Navy—Joins H.M.S. "Edinburgh"—His shipmates
described—Vourla—Malta—The Chaplain—Portsea—
Passes as mate—At home—Exeter—London—Bridport—Returns to his ship—Serious reflections—Egina
—Athens—Boat upset in a squall—Exertions in rescuing the crew—Zante—Malta—Ascent of Mount Etna—
Vourla—Sir G. Clerk, Bart.—Rev. L. H. Irving—Self-
condemnation—Portsmouth—Ship paid off, . . 12

CHAPTER III.

1837.

PAGE

Visit to Cambridge—London—Voyage to Scotland—Visits
his brother Lewis—Benefit derived—Rev. H. Melville
—Visit to Glendoick—Lockhart's Life of Scott—Severe
weather in spring 1837—Purpose of leaving the service
and settling in New South Wales — Letter from
Greenock—Ship "Portland" off Greenock—Plans and
purposes—Arrangements on board, ... 47

CHAPTER IV.

1838–1842.

Letter from New South Wales—Sympathy with his friend
in affliction—Account of the voyage—Procedure on
landing—Arrangements for his brother—Robbed in the
bush—Goulbourn—Rev. Mr. Hamilton—Description of
the country and natives—Kangaroo-hunting—Hopeful
state of mind—Mr. Waugh—Severe illness—Feels an
occasional yearning after the sea, ... 62

CHAPTER V.

1843–1844.

Again at home in July 1843, after an absence of six years—
Explanation—The Disruption of the Church of Scotland
—Appointed to H.M.S. "Volage" as Lieutenant—Old
reminiscences—Account of his new messmates—Cork
—Bantry Bay—Reference to the troubles in Ireland—
Duke of Wellington—Captain Hope of Carriden—
Derrynane—Daniel O'Connell—State of public mind

—Accident to the ship—Captain Dundas, his former
Captain—The Irish State Trials—Mayor of Waterford
—Berehaven described, ... 74

CHAPTER VI.

1844–1845.

Appointed to H.M.S. "Excellent"—Life at Portsmouth—
Change in Naval warfare—Thinks of Arctic Expedition
—Appointed to H.M.S. "Terror"—Short visit to
Scotland—Thoughts suggested by his new destination
—Greenhithe—Steam power provided for "Terror"
and "Erebus"—Account of the preparations—Strom-
ness—Whalefish Island—Natives—Last letter, . . 110

CHAPTER VII.

1845–1848.

History of facts ascertained by Sir L. M'Clintock—Mr.
Markham's account of the Schwatka discoveries, 131

CHAPTER VIII.

Officers of H.M.S. "Terror"—Probable course of events
after abandoning the ships in April 1848—List of officers
who landed at Point Victory—Summary of dates—Concluding remarks by Editor, ... 149

APPENDIX.

I. Account of the Public Funeral, January 7, 1881, . . 161
II. Testimonials, ... 166

LIST OF ILLUSTRATIONS.

Photograph of the Medal found near Cape Victory—*Frontispiece*.

PAGE

Sketch by Lieutenant Irving, explanatory of the application of steam power to the " Erebus " and " Terror,"   119

Ditto, a native in his Canoe, ...   124

Ditto, the Ships taking in Provisions at the Whalefish
Islands, ... 129

Photographic facsimile of the Record discovered by Sir
L. M'Clintock, ... 136

Map of the Arctic regions mentioned in the Memoir.

MEMORIAL SKETCH.

CHAPTER I.

JOHN IRVING, born in Princes Street, Edinburgh, on February 8, 1815, was the fourth son of the late Mr. John Irving, a much respected member of the Society of Writers to the Signet, who in his youth, and at the High School, was the intimate friend of Sir Walter Scott. This boyish congeniality is· taken marked notice of in Lockhart's Life of Scott, from which it may be gathered that Irving was a man of no commonplace mind and character. His elder brother, Alexander, Professor of Civil Law in the University, and ultimately Lord Newton, one of the Senators of the College

A

of Justice, was an eminent mathematician, and
at the same time a man of general culture.

The mother of John Irving, of whom we
are about to write, was Agnes Hay, daughter
of an eminent Engineer officer, Colonel
Lewis Hay, who was killed in the expedition
to the Helder in 1799. It is well known
that Sir Ralph Abercromby made it a condition of his accepting the chief command in
that expedition, that he should have the
services of Colonel Hay, of whose professional
skill and judgment he had already formed
the highest opinion. We mention these
facts regarding John Irving's birth and
parentage in connection with his subsequent
career and character.

His mother was the great-granddaughter
of Robert Craigie of Glendoick, President of
the Court of Session, and previously Lord
Advocate for Scotland during the Rebellion
in 1745-6. She was a very excellent, godly
woman, and had much influence, doubtless,
in the early training of her son; but she

died in 1823, when he was comparatively young.

He was eventually a scholar of the New Academy, Edinburgh, and joined it, we understand, on the day of its first opening. Some of his companions still have pleasant recollections of him. One of them, who often sat next him, mentions that he was a "nice fellow," fond of play, with a good deal of quiet humour, courageous, but very slow to quarrel or take offence.

Evidently he did not remain at the New Academy during the usual term of seven years; for he entered the Royal Naval College at Portsmouth on June 25, 1828, and in 1830, when he would be only about fifteen, he gained the second mathematical prize at that institution. It was this very medal, discovered in a lonely grave within the Arctic circle, which, forty-nine years afterwards, led to the identification of his honoured remains.

Before proceeding further with John

Irving's naval career, we may give some
account of the other members of the family.
Six sons and one daughter grew up. 1. The
eldest son, George, about ten years John's
senior, followed his father's profession, and
died, much esteemed, at a comparatively
early age. 2. Lewis Hay, a man of talent
and wide attainments, after spending some
time in Geneva, with great advantage to his
future life, under the roof of the late Rev.
Dr. Cæsar Malan, studied for the ministry of
the National Church of Scotland, and was
settled at the age of twenty-four in the
pleasant rural parish of Abercorn, near
Queensferry, and continued to perform all
his duties there, with remarkable zeal and
energy, until the Disruption of the Church
in 1843. Joining the Free Church, he was
transferred to the town of Falkirk, where he
laboured incessantly, with rare devotion, in
the Master's service, until the summer of
1877, when he died at the age of seventy.
He resembled John in many respects, and

was, we have often thought, fitted by nature,
had God so ordained his course in life, for
any enterprise demanding enthusiasm, self-
denial, and undaunted energy.   3. Mary
came next in the family. She married the
Rev. William Scott Moncrieff, an esteemed
minister of the Church of Scotland at Peni-
cuik.   She has survived him many years,
and is the mother of two daughters and of
Mr. William George Scott Moncrieff, advocate, who now fills the position of Sheriff at
Banff with much reputation.   4. Alexander
was the third son in this large household.
He entered the Royal Artillery about the
same time that his younger brother John
commenced his studies for the Navy.   He
has served his Queen and her predecessor
William IV. with distinction in various
quarters of the globe; he took part in the
Crimean war; he is a Companion of the Bath
and a Major-General; and has been spared
to act as chief mourner on the recent melancholy occasion.   5 and 6. The two remaining

sons were Archibald and David. They were
children when their devoted mother was
taken away, and therefore had few of those
advantages which the older members of the
family enjoyed. Archibald died many years
ago, leaving a widow, who still survives.
David, whose early manhood, as we shall
see, was specially brought under the influence of his sailor brother, is now a respected
Police Magistrate in Australia.

John Irving, after leaving the Royal Naval
College, in which, as we have seen, he dis-
tinguished himself, particularly in mathematics, joined for a short time the "Cordelia,"
a 10-gun brig, under Commander Charles
Hotham, in the North Sea. He then served
as a midshipman from 1830 to 1833 in the
"Belvidera" frigate, commanded by Captain
the Hon. R. S. Dundas, on the Mediterranean
station.

In the summer of 1831 his future intimate
friend, William E. Malcolm, on joining the
ship for the first time, found Irving already

there, and also another friend, George Kingston.   He too had been appointed midshipman in December of the previous year ; and
after a short leave of absence found Irving
on board on his return to the "Belvidera"
in January 1831.   Irving, Kingston, and
Malcolm were fellow-midshipmen in the same
ship from the summer of 1831 onwards.

They were drawn much together, and became mutually helpful, from the circumstance that all three were already more or
less deeply impressed with religious convictions, and had to maintain their position, as
we can surmise, under no little discourage-
ment, perhaps opposition, from some of
their shipmates.   These three youths were
together for the greater part of three years.
Malcolm left the "Belvidera" a little earlier
than the others, when she came home bring-
ing Lady Frances Hotham, whose husband,
Sir Henry, had died as Admiral of the
Mediterranean Fleet.   The ship was paid
off in December 1833, when Irving was

appointed at once to the "Edinburgh,"
then at Portsmouth under Captain Dacres.
Kingston shortly after joined H.M. ship
"Tyne," fitting out for the Mediterranean;
and thus the early and pleasant fellow-
ship of the three young men virtually came
to an end. Their several courses in life
diverged; but an epistolary correspondence
was maintained more or less steadily for
many years.

Malcolm, a son of the eminent and well-
known Admiral Sir Pulteney Malcolm, left
the Navy on account of his health in the
end of 1833. He still survives as the pro-
prietor of Burnfoot in Dumfriesshire, and has
kindly favoured us with a series of letters
which will enable the reader to form an esti-
mate of John Irving's character, and also to
trace clearly and satisfactorily the future
current of his life during the ten or eleven
years preceding his final departure in Sir
John Franklin's expedition to the Arctic
regions.

Kingston is often mentioned in the letters to Malcolm; but those written to himself are unfortunately not within reach, having been left in Canada. It will interest the reader to know that that gentleman, after being invalided from the Navy in 1839, became, like Malcolm, a student at the University of Cambridge, where he took his degree in 1846, and some years afterwards was appointed Director of the Magnetic Observatory, Toronto, and Superintendent of the Meteorological service of the Dominion of Canada; he also held, until his final retirement in 1880, the Professorship of Meteorology in the University College, Toronto.

We may now, in a new chapter, introduce the first letter of the series addressed by John Irving to his friend Malcolm. It was evidently written in the short interval betwixt the paying off of the "Belvidera" and his appointment as a midshipman on board the "Edinburgh."

CHAPTER II.

106 Princes St., Edinburgh, *May* 16, 1834.

My dear Malcolm,—I received your kind letter of 11th April some time ago, and I hope you will get this previous to your departure from Cambridge for your summer residence, which I trust you will find a pleasant one, though I am sorry to hear that you have little prospect of coming to Edinburgh.

My father had a letter from a friend the other day, saying that if I intended remaining in the Navy, I should get employment immediately. Informing me of this, my father told me that for the last twelve months he had been thinking of my going out to New South Wales as a settler, having lost this last winter, by death, almost all the friends he had of influence, and so, my prospects in the Navy having become so bad that I can hardly do worse than remain in it. My father has also been buying, or going to buy, some shares in the South

Australian Company, and hopes to get me some situation there, besides investing my own capital— purchasing land or whatever may seem best,—and also my youngest brother to go with me, and me to look after him. I have told my father that I shall be glad to leave the Navy, and that I cannot imagine the situation of a settler to be a more uncomfortable one than what I should be in on board ship with no hopes of promotion; and that I hope that I might be of some use to my brother, who has studied medicine for a year or two, and left it, and is now boarded with a farmer in the country to learn farming. As to leaving my friends and connections, though much to be deplored, *still the choice is not between going to New South Wales and staying at home, but between these and going to sea.* So, upon the whole, I think it will be better for me to go to New South Wales than to remain, for six or seven years, in a mid's berth, and then serve for all the rest of my life as a lieutenant, in the style of F., and hundreds of others. It is not fixed at all what time,—or indeed even named when,—I should set off. My father has not yet got an answer to his application to the Australian Company on my behalf.

Now, my dear Malcolm, I have laid the whole

thing before you, and I will feel thankful to you for
your advice as to what I ought to do. (I should
have told you that my father seemed glad at my
volunteering to take charge of my brother.)
Perhaps, as your brother is coming home from that
colony, you may be able to furnish me with some
useful information about what I ought to do on
arriving there, or what I ought to take with me as
useful articles, or what people there it would be
useful to me, as a settler, to get letters of introduction to. My capital will be but a few hundred
pounds. But do not give yourself the least trouble
about it; but any information, however trifling,
will be thankfully received. Perhaps some of your
brother's old letters contain information about the
settlers, their customs, servants, convicts, etc.; but
do not give yourself any trouble about it. You
may imagine that I am in a state of considerable
anxiety till it is all arranged. In going to settle
there, I must take leave of Scotland and its
inhabitants for ever; but it will be better than
being dependent on the bounty of my friends all
my life at home; and my father is an old man, not
far from fourscore, and he is anxious to have Davie
settled in some way or other. People can live
there at a very small expense. I hope you will

write soon and give me your counsel. Another
thing to be looked at is, that, as a settler, I should
have my own house, however small, and I should
be more out of temptation to sin, and be able to
lead a life fitted better to my improvement as a
Christian, than on board ship.—My dearest and
oldest friend, I am ever yours,   JOHN IRVING.

I shall be anxious to hear the result of your
examination, and your address after leaving Cambridge.

The idea of leaving the Navy and going
as a settler to Australia was not carried out
for more than four years. The writer of
the foregoing letter was about nineteen
when it was penned. It is very characteristic in the manliness, unselfishness, and
shrewdness displayed ; but the remark about
his father's age is almost amusing. The old
gentleman could not have been more than
sixty-three or sixty-four at the time.

We gather from the next letter that he
had joined a new ship, the "Edinburgh,"
then on the Mediterranean station.

TO MR. W. E. MALCOLM, TODDENHAM RECTORY,
GLOUCESTERSHIRE.

H.M.S. " EDINBURGH,"
VOURLA, *September* 24, 1834.

MY DEAR MALCOLM,—I received your letter of
the 27th July on the 3d of August, so it has been
a whole month unanswered.   I suppose you are
settled down quiet and, I hope, studious at the
Rectory after your visiting expedition to Scotland.
I am afraid it will be a long time before *Maister*
John has the pleasure of seeing the fine sights you
promise him ; however, he lives in hope.   My
father writes me that he sees no chance of getting
my promotion while the present Ministers hold
office, and says that it will be best for me to remain
afloat so long as I am a mate, as, at the Admiralty,
they make your not having served after passing an
objection to your promotion (and very properly too,
if stuck to in all cases), so I must jog on as quietly
as I can, for I cannot vex my poor old father—who
has trouble enough to provide for the advancement
of six sons in the various ways of getting a living—
by telling him of my wishes to come and live at
home.   I have seen a good deal of old Kingston,
and have taken some walks with him.   He is just

the same; and as I walked along, looking at his large shoes, swinging arms, and—although it was a hot day—an immense stiff black neckcloth, I could not help laughing and thinking how you would have been amused.

As people have become familiar in the ship, and reserve worn off, I and three others have attained to the name of saints.   There were at one time six or seven; but ridicule has made them renounce their profession and go back into the highway of profligacy and vice.   I shall mention my friends, as I daresay you would like to know about them.   Norman I have already described to you.   I found him, when I joined the ship, a real Christian in every sense of the word, and so he is to this day.   The next is a midshipman called Moil, a very wild fellow when he came in this ship, and Norman has been the honoured means of sending him to the Fountain of all mercy.   The third is a young Collegian called Fowler.   He has become very serious, and the Bible is his daily study, and he has read many of my books, beside a total alteration in most of his habits; he has been a year and a half at sea—so he had some bad ones,—but he is in earnest indeed.   He has gone through six books of Euclid with me, and we are going over them a second time; but he knew

some of them before, also Chemistry and Natural
Philosophy. He is very clever, and learns quickly;
I only hope he may retain what he acquires. The
whole of us are laughed at for reading the Bible,
and, horrid to relate, we go by the common name of
" the Holy Ghost boys." However, Norman's advice
and truly Christian example has enabled me to
conduct myself in a somewhat more Christian
way than was my wont, or rather, I have obtained
in mercy an increase of that spirit which overcometh
evil with good, and I hope all these trials will do
me good.

Poor old Kingston has been annoyed lately in the
same way. I pity him, they are so closely packed
together in a small vessel like the "Tyne." He has
a great help in the assistant-surgeon, a very pious
young man. Also Kingston has great delight in a
youngster whom he has lent a hand to, and who has
become serious. They are doing Euclid together,
and get on very well. These three are called
" psalm-singers," and old Kingston has been told
that it is quite unnatural for a young person to
spend so much of his time in reading as he does.

I was glad to hear such good accounts of your
brother. I hope some of your books will do him
good in moments of reflection and loneliness, in far

distant lands, when you can only pray for him and
hope the best. I have read an excellent book lately :
" Memoirs of Henry Martyn, missionary in India."
You will find much pleasure in reading the life of
such a truly good man as he was; also sermons by
Arnold, a Churchman, very plain and good.   We
have been cruising a good deal these last three months,
but never going above sixty miles from this, and
frequently anchoring merely for fresh beef.   We
expect to go down to Malta soon, touching at Napoli
by the way. No one knows where we shall go, as
this Admiral keeps everything so close that really
we never get two hours' waiting before sailing.   I
daresay we shall spend this winter at Malta; however, it does not much matter to me where we are.
I hope you are keeping your health, and growing
stout.   Send me your stature and weight next time
you write, and then I shall be able to judge pretty
well how your twelve months' residence on shore
has agreed with you.   And I hope you are fortunate
in your companions at Toddenham, as I suppose
your comfort depends a good deal upon their conduct.

I hope you will not think from this letter that I
am melancholy or vexed at the behaviour of my
messmates ; for I am quite happy in the knowledge

B

that in this ship[1] my own pride and bad temper have
not been the cause of their troubling me—Kingston
being situated in the same way in the "Tyne" is a
proof of this,—and that the only thing they trouble
me about is on the score of being religious; and in
such a cause it is a high honour to suffer at all.

I have the pinnace, and do nothing in the harbour
but go away in her for water, etc.   I keep forecastle
watch at sea, and we are in four watches, which
gives plenty of time for reading, which is a great
comfort to me.   I hope you will go on well, Elphie,
and work hard, that you may not be taken aback at
the College, especially in the Euclid, which you can
just freshen up in your memory a little, in case you
forget it; but I have no doubt you know what is
necessary, and don't think me officious for saying
anything about it.

And now I must conclude my letter.   May you
be a useful member of your high calling which you
have chosen.—I am ever your affectionate friend,

JOHN IRVING.

---

[1] It would appear that while in the "Belvidera" he was not
very popular on account of a hot temper and a rather domineering
manner.   He was better informed than the majority of his
compeers, had decided opinions, and was prone to become dic-
tatorial.   We can readily imagine, from personal knowledge,
that in early life such may have been his tendency.

Mr. Malcolm, although looking forward at this time to taking holy orders, did not eventually carry out his purpose.

H.M.S. "EDINBURGH,"
MALTA, *Dec.* 8, 1834.

MY DEAR MALCOLM,—I am glad to hear you are getting on so well with your studies, and that before another year has gone by you will have commenced your University course. I have always had a sort of misgiving that you would be inclined, by your friends, and by finding yourself in such good health, to come to sea again, when I know you must be so much happier where you are. I can fancy you laughing at this. However, you know that, with you, I speak just what I think, and I have no one else in the world whom I can do that to but yourself. In this ship I am on good terms with all, but intimate with none. And I am getting quite tired for want of some one with whom I might talk of something besides seamanship and points of service. We have been now lying here for five weeks, and in all probability we shall remain here until March or April. The "Revenge" has gone on a cruise accompanied by the "Vernon" and "Barham," of whose sailing she is the umpire. From what we could see during two or three days, it seemed that they sailed as nearly equal as possible, keeping abreast of each other for hours. However, it is generally thought Captain Symond's ship " Vernon " has an advantage on a wind, while the " Barham " beats her going free. There are many bets depending upon it, and their return is anxiously expected. They have had strong breezes, and it is hoped that the trial will be decisive. I suppose you are little interested in this, but I will confess I am very much, the shape of Captain S.'s ship being so different. The " Colum- bine," one of his brigs, has sailed a great deal with the squadron, and it is wonderful to see her going away two miles an hour dead to windward, under two topsails, while we are cracking on everything we can carry. The great difference seems to consist in the immense beam at the water's edge, which prevents their heeling over, and so making lee-way.

I get books from the garrison library, and read a good deal, and of all descriptions. I occasionally go to the opera. Miss Briggs's marriage with Captain Martin takes place on the 9th inst.; he has become Flag-Captain, and it is considered a good match, though he is old enough to be her father. You inquire about our chaplain. I do not know what to make of him. He makes good sermons; and as far as facts go he is a very good man; but he is very loose in his conversation, and joins in the laugh at improper jokes, and I have sometimes heard him use a polite oath. However, he is considered a very good sort of fellow. I was shocked to hear the Captain publish his intention of celebrating the Lord's Supper in his cabin the other day. He is a man very passionate, and easily put out of temper. When he is so, he makes use of the most horrible terms—old Festing was reverence compared to him,—and our Commander, a very good old man, has the same fault. Both he and the Captain hail men aloft, and express their wishes for their damnation, always adding "for all eternity." The Sacrament was received by them, and most of the lieutenants, and some of the men, one of whom got drunk the same night; and next day I heard in the ward-room enough to make me glad that I did not go, as I at first intended. I have always seen so much solemnity, and such careful preparation insisted on in the Scotch Church, that this seemed so different; and as I see I must have done harm instead of good, I thought it better not to go. I heard from Kingston some time ago; but I daresay you have more recent accounts of him. We shall probably

be paid off by this time next year, and I look forward with great pleasure to paying you a visit at
the College, where I suppose you will have a room,
etc.; but as I shall be on my way home, I shall not
trespass long on your hospitality.   However, it is
still a long time to look forward to.   I believe my
friends are trying everything in their power to obtain my promotion, but with little or no chance of
success.   But as I cannot blame myself if I am not
promoted for ten years, I do not trouble myself
about it.   I will now finish my letter with express-
ing my delight with your last.—I am, your affectionate friend,   JOHN IRVING.

The next letter is dated from No. 66
Frederick Street, Portsea, 24th February
1835, little more than two months after the
preceding one, in which he speaks of being
another year in the Mediterranean.   His
father, encouraged, as he surmises, by a
change of Ministry, had written to him to
ask leave for two or three months, that he
might pass his next examination at the
Naval College.   Captain Dacres kindly gave
him leave, he tells us, and he left Malta on

the 1st of February, arrived at Falmouth on the 20th, and at Portsea on the 22d. He had not seen their mutual friend Kingston for some months, his ship, the "Tyne," having been sent to Corfu. He adds, "however, I had some letters from him. He was quite well, and busy in doing good to every one with whom he had any influence."

The next letter may be quoted entire, as it is short, and gives an account of his proceedings while on this short visit to England :—

PORTSEA, *March* 10, 1835.

MY DEAR MALCOLM,—I received your very kind letter three days ago ; however, as I did not know my movements, I delayed writing you until I did. I passed to-day. There were eleven of us tried; nine were turned back, and two passed. I start in an hour's time for London, and from thence, per steam-vessel, for Edinburgh, my father having written me to come home. I shall be leaving Scotland about the end of the month, and will call at Harley Street for the books on my way to Falmouth,

for I must go on to Malta in the April packet; but
I shall write to you again before that time. Excuse
haste.—My ever dearest Malcolm, your affectionate
friend,   JOHN IRVING.

The letter which follows increases our
acquaintance with John Irving's character,
and informs us as to his course :—

106 PRINCES STREET, EDINBURGH,
March 23, 1835.

MY DEAR MALCOLM,—I set off to-morrow for
London, having only had a week's stay at home. I
shall be in town in the end of the week, and shall
call at Harley Street for the parcel of books for
Kingston. I hope you will give Miss S. due notice
of this, as I should feel it very awkward calling for
the books and nobody knowing anything about
them. In obedience to my father's wishes, I am
leaving home three or four days sooner than absolutely necessary for being at Falmouth by the 3d of
next month. He wishes me to call upon several
friends of his in London, whom he has written to,
and endeavour to induce them to interest themselves
as much as possible in procuring my promotion ;
but, as they are mostly strangers to me, this will be

a most disagreeable employment. Sir George Clerk
having a son coming from the West Indies to pass
is a great obstacle to me; however, having passed
all the examinations, and feeling that I have done
my best, as far as it depends on me, I do not feel so
very anxious about it. I have also to go away from
London one day sooner than I would otherwise be
obliged to do, as I have to pay a visit in Dorset-
shire, on my way to Falmouth, to Mrs. Stanley, the
wife of Captain Stanley, the commander of the
"Edinburgh." She has been long in bed, and was,
I believe, despaired of. Captain Stanley could not
obtain leave to go home, without losing the ship,
and he entreated me, with the tears running down
his cheeks, to go and see his wife before I left
England. This I promised to do. I shall stop ten
or twelve hours there, and proceed with the next
coach. The place is called Alington, near Bridport.
It vexes me to leave England without seeing you;
but it cannot be helped. However, I will take it as
a great favour if, when you are next in Scotland
(perhaps next summer you will probably be in Edinburgh), you will go and see Mrs. Scott Moncrieff.
Her name was Pringle. Her brother is M.P. for
Selkirkshire, and, I believe, she is a cousin of your
father's. She is very anxious to see you. She told

me she often carried you in her arms when you were an infant. She is a most pious, amiable lady, and I am sure you will be as much pleased with her as she will be with you. She lives at Dalkeith, six miles from Edinburgh; her husband is chamberlain to the Duke of Buccleuch, who has a palace there, so you will have no difficulty in finding her.

I have procured Newton's *Cardiphonia* on your recommendation, but I have not had time to read it yet. I shall also get, and, as you desire, consider as a present from you, the little book called *Advice to a Young Christian*.

I shall be out at Malta about the end of April, and, I am afraid, shall have some difficulty in joining my ship; but I suppose I must stick to the letter-bag. It has been an expensive business this, my coming home; but it is a great comfort to my father to think that nothing has been omitted that has a chance of getting me on. I am afraid you will consider this a terribly egotistical letter, but mine are naturally such to you.—Believe me ever your affectionate friend,   JOHN IRVING.

The next letter is dated Exeter, Tuesday afternoon, March 31, 1835. There are some

points of interest which deserve being
quoted :—

I have been endeavouring to make a little interest
for myself while in London, of which I shall give
you some account. I had a letter from Lord
Arbuthnot to Lord de Gray, written, to use his own
words, in the strongest terms he could employ. I
also had a letter from General Arbuthnot, M.P. for
Kincardineshire, to Lord de Gray, and he also spoke
to Mr. Dawson, the secretary, on my behalf. Sir
George Clerk introduced me to Lord de Gray's
nephew, Cole, the private secretary, and gave him a
note to his uncle Lord de Gray, which he said he
would deliver into his own hand, and also that he
would do what he could in my favour himself.

Some of my friends seem quite confident that I
shall be promoted in a short time, but if this takes
place in eighteen months it will happen sooner than
I myself expect. I shall leave Falmouth on Friday
morning, after post, for Malta.

I have been at Bridport to see our Commander's
wife, and remained there for a few hours, and am
now just arrived here, and the Falmouth mail starts
in a few minutes, so you must excuse this hurried
letter.

I found the poor lady quite insane; however, I saw her sisters, and have rather melancholy news to carry out to her husband, our Commander.

From having been so hurried about these last two months, and never having time to read, I regret that I am not nearly in such a peaceful state of mind as I used to be, and I am quite aware that I do not think nearly so much as I used to do about eternity and the things belonging to it. I do not know whether this may be a physical effect on the mind produced by the constant excitement in which I have lived for the last two months,—in which case, when I get settled, my mind may be restored to its former calm and comfortable state. However, it is a source of great present discomfort and uneasiness to be forced to turn my attention, with an effort, to the consideration of subjects in which I used to take great pleasure some weeks ago.

I must finish my letter in a hurry. Good-bye.—I am ever your most affectionate   JOHN IRVING.

On arriving at Malta, and joining his ship the "Edinburgh," John Irving at once recommenced his former duties. He found three letters from Malcolm awaiting him.

The two last he characterises as "real down-right scolds" for neglect and carelessness as a correspondent. This was natural enough, being written in ignorance of Irving's sudden call to England. There is a long vindication of himself in reply upon his arrival at Malta.

The letter bears date H.M.S. "Edin-burgh," May 7, 1835. After the explana-tion referred to, he says :—

But, my dear Malcolm, do not think for a moment that I am at all displeased at your scolding me ; far from it. Nothing could have pleased me more. It shows far more than any assertions could that you are really concerned about me ; and I am sure that I never read anything of yours with such heartfelt pleasure as I did these warm remonstrances on my silence and apparent neglect of your letters. Your feeling vexed at not hearing from me con-vinces me, more than a dozen letters could, that your interest in my welfare is still the same, and nothing could tend more to remove a horrid feeling of jealousy which sometimes crosses my mind, when I think it possible ; and it does seem natural, that you, surrounded by so many new and agreeable

friends and acquaintances, and cut off from all associations with your former life, should gradually
slacken your interest in, and cast off your affections
for your old friends. Do not let this remark offend
you. It is more owing to the morbid sensibility of
my own mind, combined with the long habit of deep
interest about you, that makes me feel so acutely
the bare possibility of your growing cold and indifferent about me, than that I have the least
expectation of such an event, or that you have
ever given me the slightest cause to think it at
all probable. No, quite the contrary ; and I should
be unjust to you if I did not tell you so, that it is
the greatest comfort to me to think that, as long as
we live, I have such a friend as you have been to
me ever since I first knew you, and when we first
called each other friends. Not that I am weak
enough to believe that when you and I meet again
we shall suit each other as well as when we were
in the " Belvidera." We shall not have the same
ties of situation nor the same feelings of relation
to each other as we then had. Your mind will be
filled with learning and information on many subjects of which I shall be totally ignorant. You
will feel deeply interested about many things about
which I shall be totally indifferent. All your old

associations, connected with ships and a mid's berth, shall have given place to those of a University and College scenes, College adventures, College manners and habits; while I, as habit is second nature, shall have become a sea-monster, and unable to sympathise with you in anything beyond the sphere of pitch and paint, tallow and tar.

You will have read hundreds of books of which I never heard the name; you will have studied subjects of which I never dreamt, and be intimate with many persons I have never seen. My conversation, like one who had been out of the world for some time, will seem insipid and stale to you, accustomed to the society of the cleverest and best-informed men of the age; while yours will be so much beyond that to which I shall have been accustomed, that I shall be galled by a sense of ignorance and insignificance.

I can fancy you enjoying a hearty laugh after reading all this nonsense, as you will call it; but there is many a true word said in jest, and really when I went home last I was astonished, and more so since my return, in finding myself actually more *at home* on board here than in my own father's house—so many changes had taken place there, my brothers growing up, etc. etc.

After these reflections, so eloquently expressed, and indicating a pensive mood not common at twenty, he mentions that, after a good passage from England, he had joined the " Edinburgh " on the 23d of April. Kingston, "with his old rubicund countenance," had sailed in the " Tyne " that very day for Corfu. Everything on board ship was going on as usual, and they expected to leave for Salamis on the 12th of May, to be present at the coronation of King Otho, which was to take place at Athens a fortnight later. He concludes the long letter, which was evidently intended to make up for the past shortcomings for which his friend had scolded him, in the following sentences :—

I am happy to say, that as I get settled on board this ship, I find my mind in a much more comfortable state than it was when I wrote you from Exeter. I was in such a perfect fever of excitement during my trip to England, that the devil got great hold of me, and my mind was open to all evil. I could not in that hurry and bustle " be watchful unto prayer," but being "troubled about many things, I was forgetting the "one thing needful;" but getting into my regular habits of reading and reflection has done much, through God's grace, for my soul.—I am ever your very affectionate friend,   JOHN IRVING.

H.M.S. "EDINBURGH,"
1st *June* 1835.

MY DEAR MALCOLM,—We left Malta on the 12th of May, and arrived at Egina on the 19th. I think it a most beautiful island. We remained there one day, and came here on the 22d. We are seven miles from Athens, and I have walked there twice. The place is very much improved since we were here in the "Belvidera." There are a great many new houses, and they have built a wharf and several new houses at Port Leonis, where there are a number of shipping and shore boats; in fact, all have removed from Napoli to this place.

The King Otho has been visiting the squadron, and we have been manning yards and saluting. He is proclaimed to-day on his coming of age, and the regency is dissolved, and he takes the reins of government into his own hands. Besides our squadron, there are a French liner and two frigates

C

lying here. The weather is very pleasant, and I
bathe every day. I suppose you have no opportunity of practising your swimming. I can assure
you I found the advantage of it in a signal manner
the other day. I was coming off from Port Leonis
to the ship under sail, and was under the lee of a
point where a tremendous squall came on us like
a shot. The land was not 100 yards to windward,
so we could not see it coming. Our sheets were
let go, but before they had time to render, the boat
was bottom up. I had great difficulty to get clear
from the sails, which were over my head, and pre-
vented me rising. When I came to the surface,
you can imagine my feelings on seeing only ten
people out of nineteen who were in the boat. With
great exertion we got the rest out from under the
boat and sails. There were several who could not
swim, and must have been drowned had the rest
not held them up. The boat floated keel up, and
we got everybody conveyed to her, and by crossing
our arms over the keel and holding each other's
hands on the opposite side, we held on till we were
observed and boats sent, who picked us up, having
been nearly half an hour in the water. The Captain
was very angry at me at first, but I referred him to
Lieutenant Slade of the flag-ship, to whom I had

given a passage off, and to our own pilot, an experienced man, who told him that I was not to blame in the least, and that everything had been done that could be done. It was a very sudden squall, and no fewer than five boats were upset nearly at the same time. Two Frenchmen were drowned. We were kept longer in the water, as the boats were sent away to rescue the others. I am sorry to have been led into this long account by the mention of swimming; but I am sure *that* saved my life, and perhaps the lives of one or two others whom I assisted to get hold of the boat.

We sail on the 4th for Vourla, to water the squadron. I was afraid the Captain would take me out of the boat, which is a duty I like; but he is all right now, and paid me a sort of compliment about all hands being saved.

It is evident, we think, that when the first natural irritation on the Captain's part was over, and all the circumstances inquired into, it would be seen that our friend Irving, notwithstanding his own modest account, had acted in a manner very creditable to himself, and quite in accordance with his future career.

H.M.S. "Edinburgh,"
Zante, *July* 25, 1836.

My dear Malcolm,— . . . We left Malta in
April and visited Syracuse and Catania. From
the latter place I went with a large party to
the summit of Mount Etna. There was a great
quantity of snow on the mountain, and we had
some hours' very hard work toiling up to the
middle in snow ; but we were amply repaid for our
trouble, on arriving at the top, by the magnificent
prospect of the whole coast-line of Sicily and the
southern shore of Italy laid out at our feet like a
map. As to the crater, if you could imagine a
sugar-loaf with a round hole bored in the apex of
an inch in depth and the same diameter, you have
a good model of the cone of Etna. The actual
depth of the crater is 300 feet, and the same
diameter. The edge is quite sharp, and fringed
with snow. We could sit with one leg hanging
into the crater and the other down the steep slope
of the cone, which is 1100 feet, and then the
mountain slopes away in a more gradual manner.
At the bottom of the cone the thermometer stood
16°, 9000 feet above the sea. At the top of the
cone, 1100 feet higher, it stood at 21°, owing to the

internal heat of the mountain. Water boiled at
188° at the top. We all got new skins to our faces,
from the great change of temperature in going up
and coming down. Being so early in the year, we
had to walk six miles in snow above our knees.
There were some splendid icicles hanging from the
edge into the crater—fifty feet long, and at the upper
part, three feet thick—caused by the sulphurous
vapours melting the snow on the edge.

John Irving, although alluding to the
new skins which the party got on their
countenances, as if it were an advantage,
makes no mention of a permanent injury
which his upper lip sustained from frost-bite.
It caused his lip to project, and made a
perceptible change in his appearance. Many
men would have been deterred by this from
offering themselves for service in the Polar
Seas.

We returned to Malta, and completing four
months' provisions, we sailed to Corfu; remained
there a week; visited one or two other places, and
then returned here after a cruise of a few days. We

sail for Salamis to-morrow, there to meet four French line-of-battle ships. I believe we are all going to cruise together.

Expecting that the "Edinburgh" would be paid off at Christmas, and feeling very comfortable in her, he had written to his father, asking his opinion as to his staying out on the station. It was left very much to his own wishes and discretion. As the answer showed that his remaining in the Mediterranean was not considered of any use to his promotion, he resolved to come home in the "Edinburgh." "It is nearly three years," he adds, "since I saw you last. I suppose you are so grown and altered that I will not know you when I next see you."

It would appear from the correspondence carried on betwixt Irving and his friend Malcolm, that if letters did not absolutely miscarry forty or fifty years ago, they were often much longer of reaching their destination than even the tardy locomotion of that time could explain. Perhaps this kind of

disappointment arose in not a few cases
from intrusting them, to save postage, to
friends, who either forgot them altogether
or waited for opportunities of transmitting
them on their arrival in England; because
even the inland postages were then very
high. However that may be, Irving in his
next letter alludes to a new scold which
Malcolm had given him as a careless correspondent, to which his own conscience did
not plead guilty.

H.M.S. "EDINBURGH,"
VOURLA BAY, *Sept.* 29, 1836.

I shall direct this to Toddenham, and trust, if you
get it, you will be satisfied that I am just the same
as you knew me in the "Belvidera," and that my
feelings towards you are by no means altered by
three years' absence; that I still consider you my
greatest friend, and that one of my chief pleasures
consists in recalling all that intercourse which was
almost my sole occupation and my only pleasure
while we were in the "Belvidera." I look forward
to seeing you again with much pleasure. I wrote
to my father asking his opinion concerning my

staying out on the station. He asked Sir George
Clerk,[1] and sent me his opinion. To my great joy it
was that it was more advisable for me to come
home; but if I particularly wished to stay out, I
might use my own discretion. So of course I shall
go home in the "Edinburgh." The Captain says he
expects to be paid off in January at the latest, so I
shall go on shore for a spell, having served as a
mate for nearly three years. I hope to be able to
meet you, as I shall have plenty of time, and can
come to any part of the country you like for that
purpose.

I have been very much distressed by the sad news
of my brother, the minister, having lost his wife.
She was safely delivered of a daughter, and my poor
brother wrote me by the August packet that she
was doing well, and how happy he was, and that he
would call me Uncle John for the future. But by
the September packet I got a letter from my father
saying that ten days after the birth of the baby she
suddenly turned very ill and died. Poor Lewie! he

---

[1] Sir George Clerk, whose name so often appears in these
letters, was the nephew of Mr. Irving, and therefore John's
cousin-german. He represented Midlothian for many years,
was a man of great business talent, much respected by both
parties in the State, and a trusted friend and supporter of
the great Sir Robert Peel.

had been married only four years. She was only
twenty-four years old, and he left a widower, with a
little daughter, at the age of twenty-nine.   They
seemed made for each other.   The manse of
Abercorn will no longer be the cheerful and happy
abode to which I always looked forward.   However,
I shall have great pleasure in comforting him and
diverting his mind from his loss.   The little girl too
will take up his attention; but living in a manse
for four years a life of happiness, as he did, he must
feel the blow dreadfully : but he knows whence to
derive strength and support to bear it.   But I beg
your pardon for taking up your time with what
does not concern you.—Believe me, as much as
ever, your affectionate friend,   JOHN IRVING.

H.M.S. " EDINBURGH,"
MALTA, *Nov.* 4, 1836.

MY DEAR MALCOLM,— . . . You make inquiries
concerning my books and companions, etc.   As to
books—as I have been three years in this ship, I
have long ago read all on board, the stock never
having been great.   But the truth is, that for a long
time past I have been very idle.   In our mess we
get all the magazines, *Blackwood's*, etc., the reviews,
and three or four dozen of newspapers every month,
and I must confess with shame that I have read

little else for many months past. I want you and
Kingston sadly. I smoke nearly all the evenings,
and what with regular watch-keeping and sleeping
in watches below—taking long walks—beating the
bushes for sportsmen—and constantly boat-sailing,
for which there is a sort of mania in this ship—I
have spent all this last year in a most unprofitable
manner. As to companions, I have not one friend
in the ship, although I am on tolerably good terms
with them all. And now to come to the worst con-
fession I have to make: I have no longer the same
comfort and pleasure in religious contemplation that
I have known—whether from having no one with
whom to talk to, or perhaps from gradually thinking
less and less. "The friendship of the world is
enmity with God." Ah! Malcolm, how much more
happy I was when I spoke to no one but you and
Kingston than now—hail fellow well met with
every one. I have tried again and again, and am
convinced that on board ship I shall never be
happy; I have trifled on the very verge of perdi-
tion; every day I find myself placed in situations of
every kind of peril and temptation, so that I can
hardly escape. I hear all kinds of oaths and
obscene conversation, but it does not shock my ear
now. However, the ship has commenced her fourth

year, and I hope in a few weeks more to be paid off, and my father writes me that I had better stay on shore for some time. So I trust I shall be able to refresh my wearied heart with some sweet discourse for which I long so much.

I made an attempt to make a friend of a *mid* of about three years' standing. I fancied that he had a scientific turn, and hoping, through that, to gain his confidence and have some influence with him, after much talk on these subjects, I commenced Arnott with him; but he was capricious and changeable, and after four or five weeks of great vexation and trouble, having only got with him through one-half of the first volume, he excused himself in various ways, and finally, in spite of all my persuasion, dropped it altogether, and has ever since held aloof from anything like particular conversation with me. I am conscious that I did everything I could, and, though very much annoyed, I do not blame myself. After this I sunk into my routine of laziness and trifling amusements. I daresay you will be surprised when I tell you that I spend upwards of two hours a day in smoking; but you must make some allowance for a solitary being. I also draw a little, but nothing to speak of. I count the days till the ship is paid off.

We arrived here a month ago after a passage of ten days from Vourla. Malta is as dull and tiresome and just the same as ever, except that six sail of the line lying in harbour make every place on shore constantly thronged with midshipmen.

I am so sick of the ship, and everything belonging to it, that I hope you will, on that account, excuse anything you do not like in this letter. I have no prospects of promotion. However, a few months on shore in society to my taste will relieve me much. Do you recollect my carrying you on my back down the road at the top of the harbour? I was wandering there alone and also at Bighi Bay a few hours ago: my thoughts were of you and happier days. I felt myself really alone.—Dearest Malcolm, I am ever your affectionate friend,   JOHN IRVING.

Does not the foregoing letter bring vividly before us a typical British sailor—strong in body, full of warm affections, candid and honest, aspiring after higher things, and with his heart set upon the amenities of social intercourse, to which constrained distance lent a temporary and special enchantment?

H.M.S. "EDINBURGH,"
PORTSMOUTH, *Jan.* 17, 1837.

MY DEAR MALCOLM,—I received your letter of
the 12th three days ago, and delayed writing until
I heard from home what they intended doing with
me. My father says that he thinks it better for me
to remain at home for some months. I hope to be
with you in the first week of February; but it is
not quite certain what day we shall be paid off—
the severe weather retarding us much. We were
detained three days at Spithead before we could get
into harbour. However, I think I shall certainly
get to Cambridge by the 5th at furthest. I need
not tell you how I look forward to meeting you
after our long separation. I am afraid you will
think me very awkward and ignorant. I have such
ideas of grandeur attached to Cambridge University
that I can hardly fancy that you are actually there,
my recollections of you being as yesterday, though
three years have gone by. The weather is very bad,
but it does not much matter, as I do not go to Cambridge to see it. The mention of your snug room
made me quite glad.

At Gibraltar we found the "Childers" (18). Dunlop, formerly of the "Belvidera," is surgeon of her,
and he immediately on our arrival invited me to

dine, and gave me a letter Kingston had left with him for that purpose before the "Tyne" sailed, which she unfortunately did a few days before we arrived. Kingston was quite well and happy. We shall write to him a joint letter from Cambridge. Dunlop was very kind to me. He gave me a letter to Rutherford, who is now a mate on board the "Excellent" in this harbour. He came to see me on our arrival here, and I dined with him on board his ship. He seems a sensible fellow. Both Dunlop and he desired me to remember them to you and Kingston, for whom they assured me they had a great respect, as everybody has who knows him.— Yours sincerely,   JOHN IRVING.

We are very busy, having left several on the station, and five ill with a complaint called influenza, very prevalent here. I am on my legs all day.

CHAPTER III.

THE two old shipmates met at Cambridge, and spent some days together. The following is from Irving's father's house in Edinburgh :—

106 PRINCES STREET, *March* 2, 1837.

MY DEAR MALCOLM,— . . . As you may perhaps have a little curiosity about what befell me after bidding you good-bye, I will give you a little narrative. I continued eating toast and drinking coffee until your gyp came for my things. I then went down to the Eagle, and set off from the *abode of learning,* on the top of the stage, and after a very cold ride I was put down in Holborn, and went to my cousin at Somerset House,[1] and saw the model room there. I then inquired about steamers to Edinburgh, and found there were none until the Saturday, and I was on my way to ship myself in a Leith smack, when I discovered there was a

[1] The late Charles Irving (Auditor).

steamer to Dundee, which sailed the next morning.
I then went and dined with my cousin, and slept
at the inn in Holborn.   After a rather rough
passage, we arrived at Dundee, and came here on
the top of the coach on Saturday evening, having
left you on the Tuesday morning; so I was not long
in coming, though a little round-about.

I found my friends all pretty well, and I was employed, for the first four or five days, in running
about all over the town, calling upon my numerous
aunts and cousins of every degree; and every
night I was engaged at some party or other.   All
this, though not pleasant, I submitted to with a good
grace, as it would not last long.   Last Thursday I
went out to Abercorn and stayed with my brother,
the minister, till yesterday, when he and I came
into Edinburgh, as he had some business requiring
his presence.   However, I shall soon go out and
stay with him some time, as he is very lonely there
by himself.   Poor fellow! he was so pale, and thin,
and altered, I did not know him, though he never
speaks nor seems able to bear the slightest allusion
to his wife.   He must miss her very much sitting
at his solitary fireside.

His schoolmaster had been promoted to a larger
parish, and another had not yet come.   So that my

brother was occupied a great part of the day in the
school teaching the children, and I also tried to
make myself of some little use in hearing their
lessons. He preached on Sunday, and we had
some long conversation on religious subjects; and I
feel much the better, and more able to understand
the great doctrines of Christianity. But adverting
to this subject, I cannot forbear telling you how
great good came to me from my visit to you, and
how, while with you, I felt my conscience accuse
me of the greatest neglect of religion, and how much
benefit I derived from your conversation, and the
selections you made from books for my use; and
how miserable the retrospect of my past life made
me to feel. It seems to me that I must have been
almost insane to neglect that which now seems to be
of such great and overwhelming importance. I will
always remember how, as if it had been on purpose,
Mr. Melville's text and sermon directly applied to
me,[1] and how distinctly I felt that I had been be-
witched by my own depraved imagination and the
snares of Satan. I have been reading the Bible
every morning and evening, and have found much
comfort and peace in so doing, as also from a number of

[1] The sermon referred to was on Galatians iii. 1 : "O foolish
Galatians," etc.

D

sermons I have been reading. Still, the remembrance
of my past life comes across me at times, and makes
me very miserable. But this has a good effect in
keeping me humble and mindful of what I should
be, if I had nothing but my own strength to depend
on, and how wretched I am by nature, having nothing to hope in of my own; but just the mercy of
God in Christ, as it is promised in the Gospel.

I have been reading the Bridgewater Treatises, one
of which, you know, is by Mr. Whewell; but I have
not got through them yet.

106 Princes Street, Edinburgh,
April 17, 1837.

My dear Malcolm,—As I have not heard from
you at all since I left Cambridge, I imagine you
have forgotten my address, although if I recollect
right, I mentioned it in my letter of the 6th March.
I see that the " Tyne " has come home, and is paying
off at Portsmouth. I have written to Kingston, but
have not yet heard from him.

I have been staying in Perthshire for some time
past with an uncle of mine (Laurence Craigie, Esq.
of Glendoick), and in spite of the bad weather I
enjoyed myself very much. My brother, the
minister, was with me, and remained several days

there, as he had to assist a minister in the neighbourhood in administering the Lord's Supper.   I
have had a great many pleasant walks and conver-
sations with him.   I am just going now to stay a
week with some relations in Lanarkshire, and I hope,
on my return, to find a letter from you waiting for
me.   My stay on shore is quite uncertain; but I can
hear of no prospects of promotion, or anything to be
gained by going to sea.   I find visiting very unfavourable to reading, and have had but little these
last three weeks.   Among other books, I have been
reading Lockhart's Life of Sir Walter Scott, in
which my father is a good deal mentioned at the
earlier part.   The whole country for the last month
has been a sheet of snow, and the grain, which ought
to have been a foot high, is in many places unsown,
and in many more they are still busy ploughing.
If this lasts a few days longer, there will be a famine,
they say, next year.   The accounts of the distress in
the Highlands are fearful, and it is thought that
before long it will be general.   The thermometer
goes down to 25° every night, and the young lambs
have perished in great numbers.

I hope you will write to me soon, and, if you
have fixed your plans for the summer, you will let
me know where I can address a letter to you.   I

hope you will find it possible to pay me a visit.   I
am sure you would find much in this neighbourhood
very interesting.—I am, yours most faithfully,

JOHN IRVING.

106 PRINCES STREET,
Tuesday, June 13*th*, 1837.

MY DEAR MALCOLM,—I have received your very
kind letter of the 6th inst., and I have to thank
you for your attention in procuring me the papers
relative to South Australia.   I am glad to say that
it is fixed that I am to go to New South Wales; for
the state of uncertainty was very disagreeable.   Two
of my father's old friends, upon whose interest he
principally relied for getting the promotion, have
been cut off during the past winter, and Sir George
Clerk will require all the interest he can muster to
get his own son, a mate, promoted; so, all things
considered, my father has made up his mind that it
will be better for me to leave the Navy—to which
I most willingly agree, thinking that almost any
condition is to be preferred to that of a hopeless
old mate.

My brother (David) and I purpose sailing from
Leith in a very fine vessel bound for Sydney, which
will sail about the 20th of August.   As he knows

very little about farming, and I, if possible, less, we have been advised by some people here, who have been there, to go immediately on our arrival to board in the country with some respectable settler for a year or two, before we purchase land and set up for ourselves. It appears very doubtful whether it will be better for us to settle finally in N. S. Wales, or in the new colony of South Australia; but, as I have obtained letters of introduction to several gentlemen, large proprietors in New South Wales, and as stock of all kinds is procured cheaper in the older colony, and sent to the new, it is thought the best plan for us to go, in the first place, to N. S. Wales; and, in the course of a year or two, I shall be better able to judge, and have obtained the best advice as to the best place to settle in finally. By all accounts, sheep-farming seems best adapted for those inexperienced in agriculture to engage in; and it is to that I think we shall confine ourselves. Whether N. S. Wales or South Australia is the best sheep country will be best found out on the spot. And, as I must serve an apprenticeship for a year or two, I shall have time enough to ascertain that point. As a person leaving the Navy or Army for the purpose of settling is apt to be suspected to have been in some scrape which has caused him to

leave, or, in other words, to have been turned out,
he is liable not to meet with a very favourable re-
ception as a new-comer. And I understand that
the old settlers regard every new one that comes
with an eye of suspicion, as persons who have left
their country because it was too hot to hold them.
It is therefore of great consequence to me to procure as many *credentials of respectability* as possible,
and I will, therefore, most gladly avail myself of
your offer to procure me a letter to Captain Hind-
marsh, or any other person in that quarter of the
world.

I trust we shall get on as well as many others
have done, and I much prefer having my success
depending on my own exertions than entirely on
the favour of other people. As far as my own
private happiness is concerned, I have no hesitation
in leaving the Navy. It is true I am bidding adieu
to all my relations and friends, but my only chance
of success in the Navy would consist in keeping
constantly employed, and I should be equally
separated from my friends in that case. And besides, I shall have my brother with me, and my
being of use to him is also to be considered.

My father intends giving us a couple of thousand
pounds to begin with. I ought not to have troubled

you with such a long story about it; but I should
be sorry were you to blame me for quitting the Navy.
I can assure you that in this business I have gone
quite by the wishes of my *friends*, and I was not
the proposer of it. My father says he has been
thinking of it for several months past; but this
affair of Master Clerk's clinched the business. My
brother is only seventeen years of age, and I have
no doubt that when he is four or five years older,
and has seen more of the world, he will get on very
well by himself, or, if he then wishes it, we can
remain as partners. You will think this a dreadfully
egotistical letter.—I am, my dear Malcolm, your
most affectionate,   JOHN IRVING.

This, and the three following letters of
the series, cannot fail to be read with interest, in the light of Irving's subsequent
career. They show how self-denying he
was, and how he must have persuaded himself that he disliked the Navy, while bent
upon carrying out the wishes of his father
and other friends, and doing a substantial
kindness to his young and inexperienced
brother.

SHIP " PORTLAND,"
GREENOCK, 17*th July* 1837.

MY DEAR MALCOLM,—I arrived here yesterday,
and was very sorry to find by your note that you
had been here so long kindly waiting to see me. I
regret that you had not got a letter I wrote you
from Edinburgh in time to prevent you coming
here, as the vessel was detained, and I in consequence remained in Edinburgh until yesterday. I
suppose, on your return from Inveraray, you found
letters which had not got there before you had set
off for this place. However, I take your coming
as very kind, and regret much your fruitless loss
of time incurred on my account. The " Portland "
is said to sail to-morrow; but I do not think it will
be until the day after, there seems to be so much
to do. My father accompanied us here, and has
just taken leave of my brother and me, having to
return to Edinburgh by this evening. But my
eldest brother George, whom I have often told
you of, remains here with us until we sail, so
that we are not quite alone, though I should have
much wished to have had you with me at this
time. My brother bids me say that if ever you
should be in Edinburgh, he would be happy to
see you at 106 Princes Street. He is a capital

hand, as Kingston can tell you, for showing the
lions of Edinburgh. I have got the parcel you
left on board for me. I have not yet had time
to open it. I thank you for it; it seems books.
Now, my dear Malcolm, I must bid you farewell;
I have so many things to attend to, all our things
to get on board and stow away. She is in a horrid
state of confusion. I will not fail to write you how
we are going on. I hope you will continue to be
as good a correspondent as you have been to me.
When you see Kingston remember me to him. I
was sorry he could not pay me a longer visit. I
must now bid you farewell. Remember me in
your prayers, and may God bless you. I hope we
may meet again in this world; if not, in the next.
—Your very affectionate friend,

JOHN IRVING.

Saturday, " PORTLAND," OFF GREENOCK.

MY DEAR MALCOLM,—We are now fairly settled
on board. My brother took his leave of us last
night, as we were expected to sail at three this morning; but owing to a thick fog and calm, we are still
lying about two miles off Greenock. We shall sail
to-day at high water. It is tantalising to think
that you are just on the other side of these blue

hills, but I can't get at you. I have opened your
parcel, and you could not have selected better
books. I had a copy of the Commentary from my
father; but on finding yours, I went to a bookseller,
who exchanged for my father's copy a copy of
Milton, Johnson's Dictionary, Campbell's works,
and I have kept your copy. I am very grateful
for the letters to your cousin and Captain Hind-
marsh. The latter I was agreeably surprised at.
If I had had any idea that we should have been
detained here so long, I would have come for an
hour or two to Inveraray; but, on the whole, my
dearest friend, although I have not had an opportunity of bidding farewell, still the remainder of
our lives is so short a period that although it would
have been very pleasant to take you by the hand
and say good-bye, it is not of very great consequence. May we meet where we shall part no
more, and where a friendship which began so early,
and which has been of such incomparable use to
me, may be sealed in an eternity of everlasting
love and joy among the redeemed in heaven.

Now all my *friends by blood* have bid me farewell, my feelings turn with renewed force towards
those whom God, in His mercy, inclined towards
me when I was in such need of them, and whose

steady and tried affection has been the greatest blessing of my life. I need not tell you I allude to Kingston and yourself. Do forgive me for all the unkindness and ingratitude with which I have repaid your unwearied attention and good-temper. I should have written to dear old Kingston, but I hope you will tell him about me in your next to him, and say I did not know where a letter would find him.

I feel I must confess to you a great degree of apprehension about my future proceedings, and a fear that I have undertaken what I am ill qualified to perform; and that, if I do not get on, I will regret leaving the Navy, towards the *sea part* of which I had a kind of liking. I also feel myself under a load of responsibility about my youngest brother, my father having by letter, since he left this, solemnly delivered the future care of him into my hands, and also funds for his behoof. And conscious of all my ignorance of business, and everything in fact but navigation and seamanship, I am in great fear that our affairs will be very badly managed.

As to the moral care of my brother I have fewer fears, as he seems for some months past to have taken a more serious consideration for the welfare

of his soul. However, I trust in the kindness of
God, which has already been so signally displayed
towards me.

Our ship is quite full of emigrants. In the poop
we have ten ministers, besides my brother and me;
in the second cabin fifteen schoolmasters; and in
the steerage about 200 men, women, and children.
Last night was our first night on board. All assembled at nine o'clock in the open part of the lower
deck, and one of the ministers read and prayed, after
which a psalm. The singing was extremely good,
the schoolmasters in Scotland being mostly pre-
centors, and a proper proportion of female voices.
It sounded along the water very affectingly; it
put me in mind of the Russian frigate at Napoli—
at gun-fire, a beautiful hymn which I daresay you
recollect. There is to be worship every day; and
from ten ministers we shall have a variety of sermons on the Sundays. Before going to bed my
brother and I read a little of the Scripture and
your Commentary. Our cabin I have fitted up
very nicely—a book-case, a folding-table, shelves,
camp-stool, curtain at the door. I have almost
come up to the luxury of Mr. Cooke, although I
have *not yet* got a punkah. Our cabin is the second
from aft on the starboard side under the poop, and

is well lighted by a bull's-eye over our table, at which I am now writing. I sent you a paper containing an account of a public breakfast we were at, given to Dr. Lang, who gave an account of his proceedings. I beg you will read the speeches made on the occasion.

I must now finish, or I will have to take it to Sydney.—Ever your very affectionate friend,

JOHN IRVING.

CHAPTER IV.

HERE is a letter from New South Wales, giving an account of their voyage and arrangements after reaching their destination. Mr. Malcolm and his family had meanwhile met with a heavy affliction, and John Irving refers to that in his usual sympathetic manner before entering on his own personal concerns :—

AT DAVID L. WAUGH'S, ESQ., NEAR GOULBOURN,
24th February 1838.

MY DEAR MALCOLM,—I received your letter of the 1st October a week ago, and lose no time in writing to you. Most sincerely do I sympathise with you in your affliction. I feel much for your receiving such unexpected news at a time when you looked forward to a meeting with your dear brother. I am glad to see that in the midst of your grief you do not sorrow as those who have

no hope, but take all the consolation which the
Gospel gives to those whose friends in Jesus fall
asleep.   Man was never meant by his Creator to
enjoy anything like unmingled happiness here on
earth, or how would he ever look forward with
joy to a removal to heaven?   So let us consider
that all sorrows are meant by God to give us a
distaste to this life, and a greater desire to be
removed to that world where there will be no
more tears or sorrows, no more partings of dear
brothers and friends, but where all will be eternal,
fixed, and everlasting.   Forgive me, dear Malcolm,
if in officiously reminding you of these things you
know so well, I may, instead of comforting, have
only hurt your feelings, and opened afresh the
fountains of your grief, which, when you get this
letter, time may have in some measure allayed.
It is now a year since I saw you at Cambridge;
how much has happened during that year!   Little
did I then expect to be, in a twelvemonth, on the
opposite side of the world.   Perhaps by the time
you get this letter, you will be interested by a
little account of what has befallen me since you
last heard from me previous to our sailing from
Greenock, which we did on the 24th of July.
We were six weeks to the Line, four more to the

Cape, which we passed 300 miles to the southward; five more weeks to King George's Sound, a settlement on the south-west corner of New Holland, where we were obliged to call for refreshments. The scurvy had broken out, and we had fifty people laid up, twenty of whom would not have reached Sydney alive. Two weeks' stay at this place so recruited them that we were enabled to proceed on our voyage, and in two weeks more, arrived at Sydney on the 3d of December, exactly nineteen weeks from Greenock. We lost during the passage twenty-five children and five grown persons; but notwithstanding the saddening effect of witnessing so much distress as these losses occasioned, I considered the passage a pleasant one. There was a great variety of society on board, and amongst eleven reverend gentlemen we mustered a very good library, and we used to have worship in the cabin every morning and evening. I used to assist the captain in taking his observations, and walk the deck for sundry hours daily, to the astonishment of the rest of the passengers.

The time passed very quickly, and I was almost sorry to bid adieu to the ship. She seemed the last link betwixt this distant land and Scotland, where we stepped on board.

On landing, I proceeded to get lodgings for my brother and myself, and then to deliver a few letters of introduction with which I had been furnished. I was a good deal hurt by the chilling coldness with which I was received by some, but others were kind. Every one whose opinion I asked advised me not to set up by myself as a settler, until I had obtained a sufficient knowledge of the customs of the country, and acquired the necessary experience in the management of sheep and cattle, and for this purpose they advised me to join myself, for a couple of years, with some respectable person who had been several years in the colony, and after that time I might set up by myself. The difficulty was to find a suitable person willing to enter into this arrangement. Fortunately a young man, son of Waugh the bookseller in Edinburgh (you may have noticed religious publications by Waugh and Innes), who has been four years in the colony, and to whom I had letters, was willing to allow me to join him, and take up my residence in his house, and lay out my money in sheep and cattle, to be joined with his for two years, when I shall set up for myself.

I was much puzzled what to do with my brother David, whom I had brought out with me, understanding I could set up for myself at once, and that

E

he could live with me and assist me. Mr. Waugh
objected to his living with him, as he would be quite
idle, he not having employment for so many. Fortunately Colonel Mackenzie, to whom we had letters,
introduced him to a Mr. Howe, a man of immense
wealth, who took a fancy to him, and was desirous
of making him his agent in Sydney for the disposal
of the produce of his estates, which are about thirty
miles from Sydney. I told Mr. Howe that he was
only nineteen years of age; but he thought he would
do very well. And as David himself was very
desirous, I at last gave my consent to this arrangement, although I did not much like leaving him in
the town of Sydney. He has a salary of £150 per
annum, a nice little cottage belonging to Mr. Howe,
and, as his assistant, a very respectable man who
came out in the ship with us, whose wife acts as
David's cook and housekeeper. He has now been
there upwards of two months, and is doing very
well.

    After seeing him comfortably established, I came up
here, which is 130 miles from Sydney. About three
miles from this, coming through the forest, or bush,
as it is called, the cart which conveyed my clothes
and baggage was stopped by five bushrangers, who
despoiled me of most of my wearing apparel, and

retreated into the midst of the forest. Next day we hunted on their track with dogs and black natives and a party of the mounted police, but with no success. I have now been here six weeks. We live in a hut made with upright posts, and roofed with sheets of bark. Our principal occupation is looking after our cattle and sheep, and cultivating enough grain and garden stuff for our own use. Fourteen miles from us there are a few straggling huts which they call the town of Goulbourn. Here a Mr. Hamilton, who was assistant to Dr. Macfarlan of Greenock, has formed a congregation and commenced building a church. We ride down on Sundays. I like him much. His charge is extensive, having a radius of about fifty miles. He has been only about six months in the colony.

It is a fine climate, the sky blue and clear like the Levant, which it resembles in having a hot wind from the N.W., which is fully equal to the sirocco. During its continuance the thermometer stands at 114° in the shade. In the lower part of the country it frequently stands at 135° in the shade. We are 2000 feet above the level of the sea, and it generally gets cool in the evening, the thermometer frequently falling 40° in a few hours, in which case we feel so chilly that we are glad of a fire.

It is only for four or five months that these great heats are prevalent. We live in the most Robinson-Crusoe style imaginable, all our conveniences being the work of our own hands. I made the table I am now writing on, and the bed in which I sleep. The river Wallondilly runs close to the house. It forms our bath. I had the pleasure of saving from being drowned in it, a few days ago, a young gentleman named Feild, whom I dived for and brought out in a state of insensibility. He was stopping a night here on his journey. He had been lately in the settlement of South Australia, and had been acquainted with William Malcolm there, your cousin. He said he was doing very well. That settlement is quite in its infancy yet, but I hope it will do well.

In our neighbourhood the aborigines are not numerous. The Wallondilly tribe, consisting of about thirty, pay us a visit once a month. They live by hunting, and therefore keep constantly moving over a country of about forty miles square. They live on kangaroos and opossums. I went out kangaroo-hunting with them one day. They are very scarce, and after rambling over many miles we perceived one with its small head and ears erect among the underwood. The native, to whom Mr.

Waugh had lent a gun, immediately fired and missed the kangaroo. I however, though a poor shot, managed to put a ball through him as he bounded away, clearing three or four yards at a leap. He was six feet high. The tails make good soup. The natives generally spear them by throwing at them when they come to drink, and it is only when they can procure a gun that they pursue them openly. They talk pretty good broken English, and go quite naked; but in cold weather they wear over their shoulders a cloak of kangaroo skin, which they sleep upon, with only a screen to keep off the wind, and seldom two nights in the same place. They have adopted most of the vices of the convicts; and on Christmas Day I was shocked to see a number of them lying like black pigs, dead drunk, with rum they had procured from some of the public-houses in the township. In this country, wherever there are three houses together, one you may be sure is a public, and in the township of Goulbourn, where there are about forty houses, there are eleven publics. In fact the great bulk of the population consists of those who drink rum and those who sell it.

We are fourteen miles from the nearest public, and our drink consists of milk and water, and great quantities of tea, which is very cheap. I have got a horse, and I ride into the town to church on Sunday. We have also a good deal of riding after the cattle, which range at large through the woods, and which gallop like wild deer, having so much liberty. The country consists of low ranges of hills, not very precipitous, like those in the south of Scotland; only these are covered with wood, sometimes for twenty miles without a gap. We have six convicts, three of whom go out with the sheep, and the others do farm-work. When properly treated they make very good servants, and prove faithful to their masters.

The contrast which this rural and pastoral life makes with my former way of life on board ship is very great, but I trust the season of meditation and repentance now afforded me will not be thrown away, and that my leaving the Navy will be for my spiritual good as much as it seems likely to be for my temporal,—as I see by the papers that Sir George Clerk, my only hope, has lost his election, and so could not have done much for me in the Navy. Mr. Waugh, I am happy to say, is a truly pious young man. He was brought up to the Law in Edinburgh, and has been only about four years from home. The Lord seems to have provided for

me in a wonderful way. I am in the enjoyment of
excellent health, and, excepting my separation from
all my old friends, I have nothing to complain of.
I hope your life at Cambridge will be very like
what it was when I spent that happy week there.
May God bless you in all things is my daily prayer.
—Believe me ever, my dear Malcolm, your affectionate friend,   JOHN IRVING.

The next letter is dated Sydney, May 14,
1838.

Soon after that of 24th February had
been despatched, he had a sudden, very
severe, and prolonged attack of dysentery.
His medical attendants at one time regarded
the case as hopeless; but, after a confine-
ment to bed of five weeks, he was so far
recovered as to ride to Sydney by easy
stages, which was thought the most likely
means of obtaining a perfect recovery.
During his illness he "was favoured," he
tells his friend, "with great comfort and
peace of mind, and could have died with
resignation and hope, but God did not so

will it." He found his brother David very
comfortably situated, and behaving himself
in a most satisfactory way. " I have much
reason," he says, " to be thankful to God for
all His mercies."

My dwelling is about 150 miles from Sydney. I
have 500 sheep and 20 cows, and I hope in a few
years to be, like the patriarchs of old, master of flocks
and herds. No change could be greater than from
the crowded and busy life of a man-of-war to the
solitude of the life in the bush, where you may go
forty miles and not see a living being. It is quite a
pastoral country, and we cultivate only enough for
our own use. There is a great freedom and inde-
pendence about the way of life, which is quite
pleasing. I had no idea before I came out that this
country was so completely covered with trees as it
is. If you could fancy the low rounded hills in the
south of Scotland covered with wood to the top you
would have a tolerable idea of the general features
of the country. Round the settlers' houses there are
spaces of a few acres of the forest hewn for culti-
vation. After five months' experience, I can only
say that I do not in the least seriously regret
leaving the Navy, though sometimes when I see a

goodly ship clearing the heads with a tearing breeze
I cannot help having a kind of wish to be on board
of her, there is something so cheering in dashing
along through the piping water which one never
feels on shore. I have become owner of a horse,
and have had some severe falls, which have not
much improved my taste for horsemanship. Do
you remember "tooling" out to Argos? I shall
stay here a few days longer with my brother, and
will then return to my pastoral pursuits. I am at
present enjoying the delightful sensation one feels
on recovering health after a long and severe illness,
though I am very thin and weak; it seems a pleasure
even to breathe the fresh air. The weather here is
delightful, cool and clear. How time flies and
changes take place in the lot of men! A year ago
I had no idea of being a settler in New South
Wales. I hope whenever you have leisure you
will not fail to write to me, if only a few words.
Although it is 10,000 miles distant the postage is
but a trifle, and any information will be interesting.
I am in a hurry, as the ship sails this afternoon. I
must now conclude.—Ever your very affectionate
friend,   JOHN IRVING.

CHAPTER V.

THE reader will be surprised to learn that John Irving, who had apparently reconciled his mind to the life of a settler in New South Wales, after a serious and due consideration of all the circumstances of his position, and all the leadings of Divine Providence, returned to his original profession. We cannot doubt that the varied experiences which he passed through were intended and fitted to prepare him for his future service, although there may be some difficulty in tracing the exact significance of each link in the chain of events. Having left Scotland in July 1837, he is once more under the paternal roof, as the following letter to his friend Malcolm shows, six years afterwards, in July 1843.

It sufficiently tells the story of the interven-
ing period, in the absence of other letters
which have been lost :—

<p align="right">1 NORTH CHARLOTTE STREET,
EDINBURGH, <i>July</i> 3d, 1843.</p>

MY DEAR MALCOLM,—I have just got your note.
The servant said you were to be a fortnight out of
town, otherwise I should have waited on purpose to
see you. My father had written to me, advising me
to return to the Navy; and finding the sheep-
farming in Australia a losing concern, and happening
to meet the "Favourite" in Sydney, I, through the
first lieutenant and surgeon, old messmates of mine
in the "Edinburgh," got on board as an acting mate,
the Captain writing to the Admiralty that, having
no officers to do duty, he had taken me. I had the
second lieutenant's cabin, and messed in the gun-
room. On being paid off they promoted me, dating
back to the 23d March; so that I was made Lieutenant within a year after my return to the Navy.
I am now enjoying a return home, after a six years'
absence; and it may be some months before I am
appointed to a ship. Of course, I am very glad to
have got my promotion. In Australia I lived a life
of great hardship and deprivation of everything that

is considered agreeable in this country. I had never intended to remain there permanently, but had hoped in a dozen years to come home with a competency; but when I found that I should be obliged to remain there *all my life*—no chance of making any money, sinking into a half-savage state, no one to associate with but graziers and butchers,—I had little hesitation in leaving it. I considered myself fortunate in not having got involved, as many have done, in speculations, and entangled so that they cannot leave the colony.

I was quite at home on board in a few hours. And after being a shepherd and cattle-feeder for four years, I was, in two days' time, officer of a watch, and reefing the topsails. I left my brother David in Australia. He had married well, and was so connected with his wife's relations that I saw but little of him. As I could not sell my flock on leaving, prices were so much depreciated, he will now look after them for me. Independently of the great fall of wool, etc., I was never fitted to be a grazier. I never could make a good bargain. The society of horse-jockeys, cattle-dealers, butchers, and keen, sharp, vulgar fellows, was most repugnant to me. And to get on, one must be familiar with these people; indeed, you have no one else to associate

with.   But it would require a pamphlet to explain
all to you.   Suffice it to say that wool had fallen
from 2s. 6d. per pound to 1s. per pound, and when I
had paid wages, etc., at the end of the year I found
I was a loser, and if I had remained I must have
got into debt and difficulties.

I have sunk all my patrimony there, and have but
little expectation of deriving anything from it.   You
may suppose I regret having ever gone.   I must
now go to sea again for a living; and I daresay may,
in a few years, get another step in the service.   I
shall, no doubt, be here for some months; and if
you come to Scotland this summer, *we must meet.*

I did not see Kingston.   I met old Quarles on the
street.   He told me your address, and that Kingston
was in the Isle of Wight.   Of course, you will write
me and let me know what you are doing, and what
chance I have of seeing you.—Your old and attached,

JOHN IRVING.

The following has an interesting reference
to the great events taking place in Scotland
at the time.   That one who had been for six
years absent should not fully understand
them was natural enough.

No. 1 North Charlotte Street,
August 4, 1843.

My dear Malcolm,—I got yours of the 1st to-day.
I am delighted to hear that you intend coming to
Scotland this month, as I shall, in all probability,
be able to come to Burnfoot to see you, if you write
me on your arrival there, when you can make it
convenient for me to come, and send me some sailing directions how to find your place. I have
applied to the Admiralty for employment, but have
little expectations of getting it for some time.

My brother Lewis has gone along with Dr. Chal-
mers. I never attempt to form an opinion on the
matter, as it appears quite a mystery, and so much
to be said on both sides, and the Gospel seems no
way concerned in the dispute.

I am enjoying myself very much after my long
absence from home. I look forward to meeting you
with great pleasure. But I find myself, as I get
older, more selfish, and colder of heart. I had once
a good deal of romantic kind of notions; but that
sort of thing is quite suspended, and you will find
me a much more matter-of-fact person than you
formerly knew me.

Hoping soon to hear from you, I remain, my dear
Malcolm, yours faithfully,   John Irving.

The meeting betwixt the early friends, so fondly anticipated, did not take place. The next letter explains the cause :—

H.M.S. " VOLAGE,"
CASTLETON, BEREHAVEN, IRELAND,
11*th December* 1843.

MY DEAR MALCOLM,—I am sure you will not be surprised at my writing you, though I have nothing to tell you that will be amusing; but I hope you will write me all the same, as, though it is many years since we met, I still take as great an interest in you as ever.   Here I am on board a frigate, and everything reminds me of old days.   Godden, whom you may remember a master-assistant, is again my messmate, being master of the " Volage," and Arthur Kingston (George's cousin) is one of the lieutenants, so the " Belvidera" is frequently talked of; but I suppose *time*, and being in such a different society for so long, have nearly effaced from your memory the occurrences of your midshipman's life.   But I hope you still remember me, your old friend.   I always look back to these times as the happiest period of my life, varied as it has been, and it was due to your society that it was so.   I still remember how sorry I really was when you went over the " Belvidera's " side for the last time.   Don't think

me very childish in thus writing to you. I forget
the years which have gone by, and feel as I did
when I waited for you to land at Bighi Bay, when
you were staying with the Briggs at Malta. I met
George Briggs the other day. He is a lieutenant,
and has sailed for the East Indies. Good old Kingston is getting on famously at the University. I
was very sorry to miss him in London, on my way
to join the ship at Cork. I was appointed most
unexpectedly, as I had fully intended complying
with your kind invitation to come and see you at
your border residence. She will not be many months
longer in commission, and then I hope to get a sight
of you. We and several other men-of-war are employed on the coast of Ireland. At present we are
here for some weeks as a protection to the Protestants living in the neighbourhood; but you see in
the papers about all these matters, and the military
preparations made by Government. This is the
extreme west of Ireland, and is a very wild moun-
tainous country. Many of the people speak the
English, and are quite primitive, but appear very
peaceable. I believe you are aware of how, finding
I could do nothing as a settler in New South Wales,
and being advised by my friends and promised my
promotion if I would return to the Navy, I joined

the " Favourite " at Sydney, and was cruising in her
in the South Seas for a year, visiting nearly all the
islands, came round Cape Horn last March, and on
my arrival in England found that I had been made
lieutenant.

I left my brother in New South Wales, and made
over my little property there to him; and together
with his own, I daresay he will now do pretty well.
He married and has a young family, and will want
it, as the colony has gone all wrong. When I went
there, sheep were selling at 30s. per head; when I
left, they were worth 5s. It was a very losing
concern for those who had laid out their capital in
those times when the prices were high. Though I
led a lonely life there I was very happy and con-
tented; but my father hearing how bad the prospects
of settlers had become, was so earnest in his en-
treaties that I should return to the Navy, that I
could not help embracing the opportunity of a man-
of-war at Sydney, ready, as it were, to take me home
without trouble or expense. He is an old man,
upwards of seventy, and had lost my eldest brother,
and so I was anxious to see him once again. I am,
I fancy, much in the same position in the service
as I should at this time have been in if I had never
emigrated. Indeed, I found myself not at all

F

adapted for a grazier. The buying and selling part of the business requires a man to be accustomed to dealing, and I never made a profitable bargain.

The people there are very sharp and keen hands, and many of them not very honest in their dealings. My brother there is quite a man of business, and will, I trust, be able to support himself comfortably. Now that lieutenants have had their pay raised from 6s. to 10s. per diem, one can do very well. Sir George Clerk, one of the Secretaries of the Treasury, is my first cousin, and as his son has long since left the Navy, he has no connection in the service but myself, and he has promised to do all he can to get me on, for his uncle's, my father's sake. So I live in hope of being some day or other Captain Irving. Sir George was, for many years, a Lord of the Admiralty, and has always been allied to Sir Robert Peel's party. He got me made lieutenant a very few months after my return to the Navy. During the Whig Ministry he had little interest, so I lost not much by being in New South Wales.

I saw all New Zealand, Otaheite, and the other islands of Cook, and came round the world. If I had come off scathless in the pecuniary way, I should by no means regret my colonising. I am sorry indeed that my want of success there has com-

pelled me to seek a livelihood at sea, which, even as
lieutenant, is not much to my taste. But I have
done the best I could in everything, and was quite
repaid by the glad welcome I received from my poor
old father. I have long since become quite as much
at home as ever on board ship, and my bush adventures are already fading quite into a dream.

My dear Malcolm, you must be much changed,
and I hope you will not consider me, after so long
an interval, as at all intruding myself on your notice.
I myself am the same; employed in the same way;
everything around me associated with the memory
of our earlier days. But your life must be so very
different, and your society also, that I have no doubt
you will require an effort even to recall those things
to your mind. I shall be very glad indeed to hear
from you, and believe me your attached and faithful
friend,   JOHN IRVING.

These concluding sentiments are not new.
They have been expressed repeatedly in the
course of the correspondence, and indicate a
great power of realising the changes which
time and place effect on every man ; while
they show, as the reader must have dis-

covered for himself long before this, that
John Irving was, with a dash of pensive-
ness and romance in his composition, a man
of warm affections, common sense, great
unselfishness, and genuine humility.

We have still two letters addressed to
Mr. Malcolm ; but instead of placing them
before our readers at once, we shall defer
their introduction until we have quoted the
first three letters of a series furnished by
his sister-in-law, Mrs. Lewis Irving, which
will carry us forward to his departure in the
Franklin Expedition. Those of the series
which we are about to quote cover the
autumn of 1843, and supplement the information already communicated to his friend
Malcolm.

H.M.S. "VOLAGE," 16th Sept. 1843.

MY DEAR K.,—I heard from my father that you
and Lewis were away on an excursion to Arran.
I presume that by this time you have returned to
Blackness, and according to my promise I send you
an account of my adventures since I saw you. I
was accompanied down to the pier at Granton by

a large train of friends, whom I was sorry to see fade away rapidly from sight as the steamer started off down the Forth. We had a pleasant passage, and I left London the same day. On arriving at Plymouth I found that I had to wait four or five days for a steamer to Cork. To my great joy I found the "Volage" at anchor here. I was afraid she might have gone somewhere else. I went on board direct from the steamer, and was introduced to Sir William Dickson, the Captain; rigged myself in a blue coat and pair of epaulettes; the hands were turned up, and the Captain read my commission appointing me lieutenant of the ship to the ship's company. There are three of us. I am the second in seniority. Our mess consists of seven—viz., three lieutenants, one master, surgeon, a lieutenant of marines. They are all very good fellows. I was three years messmate of one of them in a former ship, so am comfortable in that respect. We are in the Cove of Cork. Nine miles up the river is the city of Cork. A steamer goes up from here every hour. I have been up once. It is a fine river, nicely wooded on the banks; the city is a strange mixture of good houses and wretched hovels. It swarms with beggars; things are cheap, and the climate is much milder than in Scotland.

This place is something like Portobello, with machines for bathing, and is much resorted to for sea-bathing quarters. We are the flag-ship at present. The Admiral and his suite reside on shore. We have many visitors coming on board to see the ship, and many ladies do I hand in and out of boats. We are asked to many parties. The people are very frank and kind. We have no idea how long we may remain here. We may probably visit Bantry and go to the Shannon. The " Volage " has been two years in commission, and it is not likely that she will be kept more than another twelvemonth without being paid off. I shall be glad to hear from Blackness. The least you can do in return for this long yarn of mine is to send me another such account of your proceedings. You can put in something about the Kirk, as I can hear nothing whatever about it here. I am anxious to hear about its prospects. Indeed, you cannot go wrong in writing me, as I am interested in all you can tell me, no matter how trivial.—I am, dear K., your affectionate brother-in-law and sincere friend,

JOHN IRVING.

H.M.S. " VOLAGE," COVE OF CORK,
20th October 1843.

We are still employed in receiving and shipping
off provisions for the different garrisons, which are
being rendered independent of the neighbouring
country for their victuals.   More men-of-war have
come, so that with three man-of-war steamers we
make quite a fleet, and are ready at a moment's
notice to send a thousand men by steam to any
place where they may be wanted.

I think that so much preparation being made will
be the means of preventing any outbreak at all, as
they, the Repealers, seem quite crestfallen at the
cautious but firm demeanour of the Government.

One cannot help admiring the fine old Duke, who,
in this Irish business, has followed out his old plan
of providing in the first place for provisioning his
forces before sending them into the field.   For the
last four months, while every one was crying out
against the do-nothing policy of the Government,
they were quickly sending over cargoes of provisions for all the barracks in Ireland; and then,
when all is ready, they whip over ten or twelve
thousand troops, and assume the attitude of men
armed at all points and ready for everything.
There are now thirty thousand troops in Ireland

and having plenty of steamers and ships, we could attack any popular force on both sides at once. But though every preparation has been made, still it is not thought that it will come to anything. All this makes a little bustle, and keeps us from being wearied so much, lying such a terrible long time in harbour at one spell. We are likely to remain here all winter. The people are very hospitable. I could be at parties every day if I liked, but we are a good deal confined to the ship, being deficient in officers.

Since writing the above, I have had a letter from my father. He mentions that it was to be decided the following day at Glasgow [1] whether Lewie was to go to Falkirk or not, so by this time you will know all about it.

I wonder if Captain Hope [2] has any chance of getting a ship soon. I should much like to sail with him. If I had such a place as Carriden, I would never trouble their Lordships for a ship. I am anxious if some good captain was commissioning a ship to join her. I hope you will con-

---

[1] The General Assembly which had met in Edinburgh on the 18th of May 1843, met again in October at Glasgow, on account of the many arrangements rendered necessary by the disruption of the Church.

[2] Now Admiral of the Fleet Sir James Hope, G.C.B.

tinue to correspond regularly with me. Remember
me to all your circle of friends, and remember me
ever your affectionate brother,   JOHN IRVING.

No one can read the foregoing, we imagine,
without saying, " History repeats itself."
The reference to the old Duke and his firm,
well-considered policy is very refreshing.

H.M.S. " VOLAGE," BEREHAVEN,
8th December 1843.

MY DEAR KATE,—I am quite charmed with your
description of your old-fashioned house. I do
detest a new country house. Notwithstanding all
the trouble you have had, I see by the tone of
your letter that you are in better spirits than
your wont. You see there is nothing so good
for people as the excitement of a movement after
all. Your letter gave me the first news of the
departure of Alick's Mary. I hope Lewie is
pleased with your new place and its neighbourhood. As soon as you are turned a little, you
must write me again. Do not think I look for
a whole sheet of paper written full. If Lewie or
you would write even just a little note I would
be very glad, only to hear how you are, how sister

Mary and my father are, and if anything is stirring at all. I hear from no one else, and when one is among people you don't care a straw about, one takes more interest in hearing about their friends. I am now getting on for four months in this ship, and I am happy to say it is almost certain she will not be above six months more in commission. Last week the "Caledonia," a 120-gun ship, came from England to take our place at Cork, and we were ordered round to this place. We had rather stormy weather, and were five days coming. This place is a town of about five thousand people, on the north side of Bantry Bay. An island, six miles long, lies off the town, and the harbour is the passage between the island and the main. This island is the property of Lord Bantry. He has given the officers leave to shoot over his estates, and the game is most abundant—hares, woodcocks, and snipes.

The people are, almost without exception, Roman Catholics. There is a Protestant curate, but he was nearly killed the other day, and I daresay he, and whatever Protestants there are in this neighbourhood, are very glad to have the "Volage" lying at their doors. We have also a man-of-war steamer with us. There are now, on this Irish coast, 1 line-of-battle ship, 3 frigates, 11 steamers, a brigantine, and a cutter, all dispersed on this south-west coast. Several are in the river Shannon. We are only about ten miles from Derrynane, Dan O'Connell's property and country house. It is a very fine place, quite like a nobleman's; but it looks like catching him, putting down a man-of-war just at his door. The people, even Dan's own tenantry, are very civil to us, and all the gentlemen, of all creeds, have invited us to their houses, and given us the use of their horses; indeed, the rough, hearty hospitality of the gentry of the far west is quite Highland, and the half-warlike state of their households is quite picturesque. It is shocking to hear the cool indifference with which even the ladies mention a man being waylaid and murdered, a house burned, or a notice to prepare a coffin written in blood; they are quite used to these. Lord Bantry had one sent to him the other day. I am told that he and some others in this district applied to Government to protect them. We could land, if wanted, nearly 200 men from this ship; but they say that even the name of our being here has given the greatest confidence, as they had begun to fancy they were neglected by our Government. Since I wrote this, another man-of-war steamer and the cutter have arrived with thirty additional marines on board. These vessels will be

stationed here along with us. We could amongst
us turn out 300 men. There are some copper
mines not far from here, at which there are upwards
of 1000 people employed. I am going to them.
The country really swarms with people. Even on
the high rocky hills, it is all little square fields of
one or two acres, like a chess-board, and dotted with
cottages, or rather huts, every one of which is full of
children. Wherever a potato will grow it is planted.
Boats full of people of both sexes and all sizes are
hovering round the ships all day, staring their eyes
out. As they are by no means well off for clothing,
and mostly bareheaded, and talk in a language of
their own, it reminds me much of being surrounded
with canoes full of staring and jabbering natives in
the south seas. Write me soon, my dear Kate. I
don't care about its being a long letter. Just let me
know in your own way how you are all getting on.
Love to Lewie and Mag.—Your affectionate brother,

JOHN IRVING.

H.M.S. " VOLAGE,"
PLYMOUTH, 14*th January* 1844.

. . . Our ship was taken into dock on New Year's
Day, when it was found that she had knocked off
32 feet of her keel, besides scraping off a good deal

of the copper sheathing. A man-of-war is built double, so as long as only the outside case is injured she cannot leak. She was taken out of dock yesterday, and will be ready for sea on the 20th instant, when she will, we expect, return to Ireland. Government keep adding to the force in Ireland. We are curious to see what may be the effect of the pending trials. I dined the other day with the Captain's mother, Lady Dickson, and met some very nice people. She is a fine old lady. We have now got the ship alongside of the hulk, and are busy getting everything on board her again that had been taken out to lighten her to go into dock—guns, provisions, and a great flitting entirely.

I had a letter from Aunt Jane on New Year's Day. The old lady is a capital correspondent. She had a little to say about every one of my friends, and all in a short pithy style much to be admired. I do not expect to be above ten days longer here, but hope to hear from you or Lewis before we leave. My kind regards to my friends at Grange.—Your very affectionate brother,   JOHN IRVING.

The following letter to his friend Malcolm, of a few days' later date, may come in appropriately here :—

PLYMOUTH, H.M.S. "VOLAGE,"
January 27, 1844.

MY DEAR MALCOLM,—I was very glad to get your
letter of the 20th instant, as I was afraid you had
not received mine. As to your quite forgetting me,
I never thought of such a thing. I am very sorry
that I did not see you at all when I was on shore,
as I will not have another opportunity for some
time. The "Volage" is now ready for sea—sails
bent, etc.,—and we are daily expecting our orders.
Our probable destination is the Irish coast, as the
ship's time is up next August. We had not suffered
much damage by getting on shore in Bantry Bay.
When she was taken into dock, we found 32 feet of
the false keel, and a small piece of the main keel,
had been knocked off. We have spent a month very
comfortably in Plymouth on board a hulk, and feel
the change back into the ship very disagreeable,
owing to her having been fresh painted.

I rather like being in Ireland ; indeed, anywhere
on the home station is a novelty to me, having been
so many years away from everything English.

If you are at Burnfoot next summer, I daresay,
on the "Volage" being paid off, I may be able to
make out a visit to you. What a pleasure I anti-

cipate in going over all that has befallen us since
we last met, and in recalling those days when you
used to be everything to me! Guess whom I met
the other day?—Cook the carpenter, whose cabin
we used to go and read in. He was looking old
and feeble, and hardly recollected me. He is in
some ordinary ship here.

I quite agree with you in your sentiments about
the Kirk matters, of which I heard much *pro* and
con. during my short stay in Scotland. My brother
has been called by the Falkirk people, and is now
the *Free* man there. I was very sorry to find he had
given up his parish; it was such a beautiful place
on the Forth, only twelve miles from Edinburgh.
I hear very bad accounts from my brother in New
South Wales of the embarrassment and distressed
state of matters there. I am afraid that he also
may be a sufferer. I have every reason to be glad
I embraced the opportunity of returning to the
service offered to me there, and that I did not persevere in a hopeless pursuit for which I was unfit
from my previous habits. Had I gone out there
six years sooner I might have done well; but the
day was past, and if I had been serving as a mate
all the time, I believe I should not have been made
lieutenant above a couple of years sooner, so I did

not lose very much in the Navy. I must now *stick
to it*. My only interest is Sir George Clerk, Secretary to the Treasury. He has no other connection
now in the service, so I must try before another
change in the Ministry to get made Commander;
for a lieutenant's half-pay, 4s. per diem, is rather
too small to retire upon. I am so used to the ship
life that it comes quite natural to me, and I seldom
find myself thinking about the shore. I expect
next summer to have two or three months' run on
shore when the " Volage " is paid off.

I was very glad to hear such good accounts of
Kingston, our old friend. His success, however, is
nothing but what I expected. He has a great deal
of energy and perseverance, besides no common
ability. I will send this to Burnfoot, and write
you in what part of Ireland we are likely to be
stationed, in a few weeks' time.

I delivered your message to Godden. He said
that he remembered you, and that you were a nice
little fellow. What changes do ten years make !
How queer you must feel on going on board ship !
There is a great difference however betwixt being
the Captain's guest, and belonging to it. Do you
remember the names and uses of the different ropes,
sails, etc. ? I daresay you do. I know that I

remember things which happened ten or twelve years ago better than those only five or six years ago. How you must have enjoyed revisiting the Mediterranean! Were you in Greece, or at Malta, or any other place where we had been in the old "Belvidera"? I met Captain Dundas in London; he was very kind. I have never met his equal since. He was in all respects a perfect officer and gentleman. I must conclude for the present.— Always your affectionate friend,

JOHN IRVING.

I have had some thoughts of joining the "Excellent" if I can, as I believe it is a help to being promoted.

H.M.S. "VOLAGE,"
PLYMOUTH, Jan. 31, 1844.

MY DEAR KATIE,—Glad I was to get your letter. I am pleased to hear that you are settled in your new abode, and likely to be comfortable there.

We sail to-morrow for Cork. Government have been a little anxious about the effect of these trials. Three or four more regiments are ordered off; two companies of the Royal Artillery and some ships. But it will all end in nothing, now that the lawyers are mixed up in it. We spent five very pleasant weeks at Plymouth; which has made a great hole

G

in the winter. Five or six weeks will soon pass away, and then I hope to come and see you all at Dorrator. It will be no novelty to us going back to the Paddies; most likely we may be sent round to Bantry Bay again. I continue satisfied with my position on board. We have a nice set of fellows in our mess; agree well together, and have no quarrels, which is everything on board a ship.

Give your little daughter a kiss from Uncle John. What is her name?—Your very affectionate brother-in-law,   JOHN IRVING.

H.M.S. " VOLAGE,"
COVE OF CORK, February 24, 1844.

MY DEAR KATE,—We were eight days coming round from Plymouth, the weather being very bad; in fact, a succession of gales, with rain and snow. We got here on the 9th, and have every prospect of remaining until summer. Our life is monotonous in the extreme. The large ships have been with-drawn, and the " Volage " is again the flag-ship, and our principal occupation is boarding all vessels entering the harbour, and reporting particulars to the Admiral, who lives on shore.

There is very little doubt we shall remain here till our period of commission expires, about August

next, when I hope to be able to come and stay with
you a little time.

You know as much as I do about the State trials.
Those Irish I have conversed with seem to think
that the priests will never let the people alone until
they either get the repeal or have a rebellion. It
is universally looked upon as a religious question.
One idea seems common among the lower classes,
that if they should rise, they will immediately receive
assistance from America, who could attack all our
Canadian possessions at the same time. They consider it certain they will get repeal, and have Ireland
for the Papists before long, by some means or other.
If Sir Robert Peel is supported, he will weather
them all ; but I was sorry to see the cordial recep-
tion given to O'Connell by the Whigs in Parliament.
As long as they increase the difficulties of the
Government they don't care.—Your affectionate
brother,   JOHN IRVING.

It is just one year since I sailed from Sydney for
the last time, and I have only received one letter
from David, which you saw.

It will be seen from this that although
John Irving joined the " Favourite " at

Sydney, he had returned thither, after cruising in the Pacific, and before finally sailing for England.

COVE OF CORK, 20th March 1844.

Things go on here in a quiet, regular way. We are anxious to know what sentence will be passed on Dan O'Connell. We are flagship, and it appears probable we shall remain here until August. We have had many gales lately. A melancholy accident occurred at Tarbert. A young lieutenant Nichols, commanding the dwarf steamer, observing a boat drifting out to sea with one man in her, during the gale, put off in his gig to board her. He had not gone far when his gig was capsized, and he and one man were drowned. He had been married only two months, and his poor wife was on board his vessel and watching his progress. She was a beautiful young creature, and her distress on seeing the boat disappear cannot be described. The bodies have not been found. One of our lieutenants has taken the command of the steamer.

H.M.S. "VOLAGE,"
COVE OF CORK, April 10th, 1844.

MY DEAR KATE,—. . . Our days are spent very much alike. We take the same walks and meet the

same sort of people every day. We are the flag-
ship, and appear likely to remain here at anchor for
some time to come. You will, I daresay, see in the
papers an account of a grand dinner given to O'Connell
the day before yesterday, at Cork. We had some
fun with the Mayor of Waterford and his Radical
Corporation. They had hired a steamer to bring him
round from Waterford to attend this dinner. They
entered this harbour, with band playing and a flag
with "Repeal" on it: this the Custom-house had
made them haul down. Yesterday on their return
to Waterford, they came down from Cork with band
playing and large flag at their mast-head, with the
Waterford arms on it. They passed close to us, and
we hailed them to stop, and on their not doing so,
we fired a gun, which brought them to a stop at
once. We sent a boat and hauled down and brought
away the flag, to the great disgust of the Mayor and
body corporate, who proceeded down the river shorn
of their decorations. We retain the flag, which is
very large, with city of Waterford arms in the
centre : viz., three lions and an indescribable thing,
meant I suppose for a fort, and a Latin motto,
" *Urbs intacta manet Waterford.*"

A large mob of the *pisantry* had assembled in
the principal square, just abreast of our ship, to

cheer the Waterford Corporation on passing. On
firing the gun, the mob fancying it was meant to
disperse them, and that a 32-pounder shot was at
their heels, ran in all directions, tumbling over one
another in their hurry, and allowing the crest-fallen
Mayor and Corporation to proceed without any farewell shout. I hear that a thousand people were at
the dinner; but I daresay you will see all about it
in the papers.

I am looking out anxiously to get another letter
from David, as the accounts by the last were so
unfavourable. I more and more regret ever having
gone there—so much time and money thrown away,
so much hardship gone through to no purpose.
However, it is of no use fretting about what is past
and irrecoverable. "Enough for the day is the
evil thereof" is a maxim we sailors adopt as the
groundwork of our philosophy, and—but I must
not scribble nonsense.

The weather here is beautiful. We have had
no snow or great cold such as you in the north
have had. The spring has set in, the trees are in
bud, and everything green, and like what it will be
with you in the end of May. We are rather curious
to know what effect putting O'Connell in *chokey*
(Botany Bay for jail) may have. We hear that two

line-of-battle ships are coming before the 15th.   In
that case we may be sent to one of the smaller
harbours on the west coast.   We are glad of anything to make a little change, and call this lying in
harbour doing garrison duty,—our being like little
more than floating barracks, some having troops
living on board.

I have inflicted a terrible long yarn upon you ;
but in your last you said you were *solitaire.*   So
you will have leisure to spell your way through it ;
and I trust you will follow the good example I have
set you, and send me soon a similar infliction.
—With love to all and sundry, believe me, dear K.,
your affectionate brother,   JOHN IRVING.

We now give the last letter which Mr.
Malcolm has preserved :—

H.M.S. " VOLAGE,"
BANTRY, *June* 1, 1844.

The sight of your well-known handwriting did
my eyes no small good this evening.   Do not suppose that I make the slightest allusion to my seeing
it seldom.   The fact is I am really surprised, when
I think on it, to hear from you at all.   It is now
such a long time since we parted, that it is quite

contrary to all the known effects of time and absence, to suppose that much correspondence would pass between us. The more so, as you are living among people who are all strange to me, and occupied with pursuits quite out of my way; and I also similarly situated in respect to you. As you refer to our old castle-buildings which gave us so much amusement during our many nightly pacings of the weary deck,—I often think of them, when I fancy to myself you turned country-gentleman, and settled on shore. Ignorant in the extreme as we were (I ought to speak for myself however) of life in all its ways, excepting a mid's berth, I am no way surprised to learn that your country abode cannot realise our delightful conceptions; but I daresay you forget half of them. I do at all events. I remembered them well when I used to be trimming my lonely fire of a winter's evening in Australia; but I wanted only your dear individual self to fill up the scene, and we should many a time have had to the life our half-savage features of domestic happiness acted over, with everything around in unison with our airy planta- tions of old. As it was, *solitude* was none of the parts thereof, so I in disgust, after four years' trial, walked the deck again. However, I learned that

there are "many things in a farmer's life not
dreamt of in our philosophy." But your farmer's
life, I daresay, bears no resemblance to my bush
experience, and I doubt not you are enjoying
yourself very much.

You ask me about our doings. Of these I can tell
you very little, as we have been generally doing
nothing. We have been backwards and forwards
between Bantry Bay and Cove of Cork for the last
six months. We were a month at Plymouth at
Christmas. We have been here for some time
back ; and as the ship's time expires next month,
we expect soon after that to be paid off. For some
time I have been trying to get appointed to the
" Excellent " gunnery ship at Portsmouth. I have
great hopes of succeeding. If so, I shall be there
upwards of a year, during which I am most sanguine of seeing you. Should I not get appointed
to the " Excellent " previous to this ship being paid
off, immediately on that event I shall take a run
down to Scotland and be there on half-pay until
I get some appointment. At all events, it is un-
likely I should go abroad without seeing you.
Last August, if I had not been suddenly sent
to this ship, I should have paid you a visit at
Burnfoot. But, my dear fellow, it will not be

my fault if I do not see you, if I get a chance at
all. You are my earliest friend. I never knew the
meaning of the word until I met you, and I have
met no one since to whom I could feel so much
attached; and there is little in this world would
give me so much real hearty pleasure as giving
you a squeeze of the hand. I had a letter last
week from our mutual friend, dear old Kingston.
He is at Cromer for the vacation. The kind,
honest old fellow: he heard that I had a cousin—
a youth of some seventeen or eighteen years—going
next term to Cambridge; and he writes to me offering to *chaperone* the lad, and says he will give him
a lift. He seems in good spirits. He mentions
his having got at his last examination the second
prize. He seems delighted with the sea-side.
What a steady, persevering honest fellow he is! I
shall write you, without fail, should I get appointed
to the " Excellent," or if this ship should be ordered
to England to be paid off. These are the only
changes likely to occur affecting my movements.

My time is spent in the routine of duty apper-
taining to a lieutenant of a 26-gun ship, varied by
walks on shore and returning the calls of the
residents in the neighbourhood, who are almost
oppressive in their hospitality. It is hard to com-

pose a letter out of such materials, so excuse this
composition.—From your affectionate,

JOHN IRVING.

This, as already mentioned, is the last
available letter to Mr. Malcolm. That the
two friends ever met is doubtful since 1837,
when Irving departed for Australia.

We may now resume his story, as detailed
in his letters to Mrs. Lewis Irving :—

H.M.S. "VOLAGE,"
BANTRY, *June 19th*, 1844.

I have just got your kind letter of the 10th instant.
We came round here from Cork last week.   So far
from the imprisonment of Dan O'Connell rendering
the presence of a force no longer necessary in Ireland,
there seems a greater ferment than ever amongst the
Irish.   Meetings have been held in every small
town, and most inflammatory language made use of,
and the Protestants scattered about in the south
have been much alarmed.   We are at the head of
Bantry Bay, within a quarter of a mile of the town
of Bantry.   The bay is about twenty miles long,
much like the Firth of Forth ; but it is much more

precipitous at the sides: hills very high break down
at once into the water. One of them is 2160 feet
high. The appearance is rocky and barren, except
just where we are moored, where the ascent from
the sea is more gradual. The mansion of Lord
Berehaven is within a few yards of the beach, and
just abreast of the ship, almost within hail. It is
an old-fashioned, flat-roofed, square house, about the
size of Captain Hope's, faces the sea, and has a green
slope in front down to the water. A park, with deer
and a good deal of wood, stretches away on the rise
behind to the foot of the mountains. Just outside
the park wall is the village of Bantry, a small, dirty
place. I believe we are here as much for the special
protection of his Lordship as anything else, he having
had threatening letters sent to him. We have a
man-of-war at almost all the sea-ports of the south-
west and east coasts of Ireland. We are quite uncertain about being paid off. However, I expect to
pay you a visit before the end of the year at farthest.
During the last six months we have had a nearly
new set of officers in the "Volage," and we are much
more comfortable than before, the Captain agreeing
better, and everything going on smoothly. I had a
letter about a week ago from my Aunt Jane, so
your news was all forestalled. However, I am

always glad to hear that you are all well and happy, even if you say nothing more.   My warmest re-membrance to all friends, and believe me, dear Kate, your most affectionate brother,

JOHN IRVING.

CHAPTER VI.

THE next letter is from the "Excellent." We saw that he had made up his mind to spend some time, if possible, in that ship, with a view not merely to accomplish himself more thoroughly in his profession, but also to strengthen his claim for promotion. The exact date of his entering the "Excellent" does not appear, although it was probably in December 1844, a short time before the "Volage" was paid off at Plymouth.

H.M.S. " EXCELLENT,"
February 12, 1845.

MY DEAR KATE,—As I don't wish to get another scold for being remiss in writing, I have a letter under weigh, though I have nothing very particular to tell you. I had a letter last night from my father, and was glad to hear all my friends are well. I am very comfortable on board this ship, as far as comfort

of accommodation and a good mess is concerned.
We have generally twenty at dinner, and our ward-
room is carpeted, and a stove in it, so it is very
snug for the winter. I regret Ireland very much.
I know some people there I liked very much, and
with whom I was quite at home. That is the great
evil of a sailor's life; he has always to bid farewell.
I do not know a single creature at Portsmouth, and
have no inducement to go on shore, and seldom do
so. I attend an Independent church; just like the
Scotch, only they sing Dr. Watts' hymns instead of
the Psalms. The Free Church deputation had the use
of it when they came here. Our chaplain preaches on
board in the forenoons, and I go ashore in the after-
noons. During the week I am busied in various duties,
and have not much spare time. There is a constant
drilling at great guns, and firing shot and shell at
targets, going on here, preparing the men previous to
their being sent to sea as gunners. Gunnery is now
being paid much more attention to as a scientific
art. Should there be another war, more will be done
by steam and proficiency in gunnery than by the
old, though more dashing style, of going alongside
the enemy. I have a night-watch to keep every
other night, of four hours, but I don't dislike it, as it
is *solitary*, and I think of old times and of my absent

friends. It is now three years since I quitted the *bush* and rejoined a man-of-war life, so totally different, that on looking back it seems quite a dream. I have not heard from David since the last letter which Lewis saw. I hope you get good accounts from your brother. I shall be glad to hear from you, my dear Katie; I have always felt you were very kind in taking the trouble of writing to me, whom you did not know much about; and I hope that any neglect, which was not intentional, will not lead you to write seldomer than you did. Indeed, it was the leaving Ireland, the journey here, and so on, that put it out of my head. I had, on arriving here, mentioned to my father that I should like to go on a discovery voyage to the Arctic regions, *which is now being projected.* I have just heard from him that he had informed Sir George Clerk of my wishes, and had got no answer. So I am waiting the result. It would give me a chance of promotion, on returning after two or three years, and would, at all events, be a change of scene, a relief, and, if one came back, something to talk of. I see my old ship, the "Volage," was paid off at Plymouth last Saturday —With love to dear Lewis, believe me ever, dear Katie, your very affectionate brother,

JOHN IRVING.

H.M.S. " Excellent,"
Portsmouth, *February* 28, 1845.

My dear Katie,—Many thanks for your very
kind letter. You see I am determined to give you
no chance of indulging in a scold. I am still in
suspense whether or no I am to go on the Arctic
Expedition. I shall be glad to be put off *it*, as it
affects my prospects for the summer very materially,
there being some difference between the regions of
thick-ribbed ice and perpetual snow, and the green
fields I might visit if I did not get appointed, for
I had some idea of coming down to see you then;
but I imagine going would probably assist me in
getting advancement in the service; and in the
usual routine there is but a poor prospect. I do
not believe I have much chance of going, so your
wicked wishes are likely to be gratified. It is not
a service of much danger, and they take provisions
for only two years; so they must come back in that
time, if at all. The "Excellent" is very comfortable;
but it is a tiresome kind of life, and Portsmouth is
a nasty place. I want something more exciting,
and not to be lying in a harbour. It is now nineteen months since I last saw you. It seems a long
time. Give my kindest love to Lewie; I suppose

H

he is too busy to write to me ; your letters of course tell me everything he could tell me.—I am ever, my dear Katie, your very affectionate brother,

JOHN IRVING.

The next letter leaves him on board the "Terror." He had gained the object of his ambition by being appointed one of the officers to accompany Sir John Franklin in his Expedition to the Arctic regions :—

H.M.S. "TERROR,"
WOOLWICH, 18th April 1845.

MY DEAR KATIE,—Many thanks for your very kind letter of the 11th, which would have been replied to before now; but I did not get it owing to one of our fellows taking care of it for two days instead of telling me of its arrival. As you say, my visit was one of the shortest, but better that than none at all. I can assure you there was no one it grieved me more to part with than yourself; for somehow or other, from the very first time we met, you and I seemed to understand each other wonderfully well. I got back here on the Monday morning to breakfast, and went about my occupations as usual. We make some show now, having got the masts up and rigging complete, ready for sea, and are now busy stowing away everything, provender, etc. etc., for two years' consumption. They talk of sailing on the 1st of May ; but I suspect it will be some days later. As you observe, there must now be a *long blank* in our correspondence. However that may be, I hope when we meet next we shall not be obliged to part so quickly. . . . Whatever happens, it is the will of God.

I hope you do not think me so weak as to labour under any presentiment of evil ; but remember this is no common voyage, and two years is a long period to look forward to in the life of the healthiest and the least exposed to risks. Only one half of Sir John Franklin's former party returned with him, and our " Terror " in her last voyage with Captain Back was so crushed by the ice that she could not have been kept afloat another day, when they got into Loch Swilly. Two years is a long time without any tidings, and perhaps we may be three years at least. Do not give us up, if you hear *nothing*. But now I will throw over a new leaf with the rest of my letter, and tell you that I am very sanguine of succeeding in the object of our expedition. Everything has been done that the latest improvements in the various branches of arts relating to nautical matters could suggest; and every preservation against the climate provided for the health and comfort of the crews; and we must for the rest put ourselves, and, what is dearer, our hopes, into the hands of our Maker. Should it please Him to permit us to return to reap the fruits of our labours, I trust the greater the dangers we may have passed the more gratitude we may be enabled to show in our future lives for the protecting Hand without which, after all, our skill and devices and contrivances are in vain.

I intended to write something to amuse you, but I find I cannot help being serious. Everything around me, and every duty I am engaged in, tend at present to make me so,—I mean all keep so much alive the feeling of a long separation from those near and dear to me. Even in writing I am reminded that a terrible long pause of anxious suspense is before me, when I can only hope, without a prospect of tidings of good or ill. So, my dear Katie, do not blame me that you should have been, whilst reading this mass of scribbling, obliged to banish your usual smiles. I will write you yet again, so I shall not take a very formal farewell of you this time. My most brotherly love to my dear Lewis.—Yours very affectionately,   JOHN IRVING.

H.M.S. "TERROR,"
GREENHITHE, *May* 16, 1845.

MY DEAR KATIE,—I have sat down to bid you
farewell, for we sail to-morrow on our voyage. We
came down from Woolwich to this place, which is
near Gravesend, two days ago. We have been
detained by some preserved meat not being ready.
We take two years' provisions, and a transport
accompanies us with a third year for each ship;
so if you do not hear of us for three years, you
need not think we are starved. We tried our
screws, and went *four* miles an hour. Our engine
once ran somewhat faster on the Birmingham line.
It is placed athwart ships in our afterhold, and
merely has its axle extended aft, so as to become
the shaft of the screw. It has a funnel the same
size and height as it had on the railway, and makes
the same dreadful puffings and screamings, and will
astonish the Esquimaux not a little. We can carry
twelve days' coal for it; but it will never be used
when we can make any progress at all by other
means. We have the same spars and sails as
before; but Parry found that during the few days
the sea was a little clear of ice he had no wind;
and we hope then to feel the power of our screws.

It is thought probable that we shall pass the winter near Melville Island, and next summer try to get westward to Behring's Straits. See the Map. I think we shall be all *bons compagnons de voyage.* I like my skipper very well, and nothing seems to be left undone in the way of providing for our wants and comforts. We have a large hand-organ in each ship. One plays fifty tunes, ten of which are psalms and hymns. We bought it by sub-scription. "Music has charms," you see. We are laden as deep as we can swim; and I hope we may have good weather crossing the Atlantic in this state. We must, like mice in a haystack, eat away and make a little room for ourselves.

Our decks are crowded with casks, and even the cabins are nearly filled up. However, as our Captain says, we have not shipped for comfort. We are all most sanguine of success. I am afraid, however the voyage may terminate, that I shall have little chance of promotion, as I am the junior lieutenant, and there are three in each ship, and it is hardly to be expected that they will promote them all. I daresay that long before I return you will be quite snug in your new house. Excuse this, but I have much to occupy me for the rest of our stay, which is only a few hours. We shall pass the Orkneys, and perhaps, should it be foul winds, may anchor at Stromness. Now, my dear Katie, I shall bid you farewell. I shall let you know our position and prospects in August when the transport leaves us.—My kindest love to Lewie, and believe me ever, my dear Katie, your most affectionately,   JOHN IRVING.

The accompanying sketch, showing the adaptation of locomotive machinery to the

Adaptation of Locomotive Machinery to the Ships.

ships, was sent with the foregoing letter of May 16, 1845. It is interesting in connec-

tion with the great and rapid progress since
made in nautical steam machinery.   With
this primitive use of steam ; the heavy-
laden condition of the ships ; and the almost
certain inferiority of the preserved food at
that early period, we cannot help fearing
that the Expedition must have laboured
under considerable drawbacks and disad-
vantages.

H.M.S. "Terror," Stromness, Orkney,
Monday, 2d June 1845.

My dear K.,—I suppose you know we left the
Thames this day fortnight.   On our way to the
north we have had a bad passage, getting here only
on Saturday night.   We had steamers to tow us,
but off the coast of Suffolk it blew so hard that we
had to anchor.   We then got separated, and got here
as we best could, it being our appointed *rendezvous.*
The steamers came here, two days before us, looking
for us, and then went back to Aberdeen and picked
us up off there.

We start again to-morrow, having watered and
repaired some damages, also replenished our live-
stock on board the transport, four of the oxen having
died from the weather and pitching of the vessel.

The Orkney people are very kind, and think they cannot be too civil to us. We made a great show in the harbour of Stromness,—two men-of-war steamers, our two ships, and the transport. The third steamer was obliged to return, having suffered considerable damage at the beginning. We are all well and in good spirits; and, I believe, notwithstanding our delay, we shall be in Baffin's Bay quite soon enough for the clearing away of the ice, which does not break up before July. I shall write you by the transport when she leaves us, as that will be the last opportunity of writing for a long time. We have had very fine weather for the last six days, and it looks likely to last, and afford us a good passage to Greenland. This is of some importance on account of the cattle and sheep on board the transport, as we can get no further supplies after leaving this place. We are commanded by a fine old fellow, of whom you have read, I daresay, eating his own boots—Sir John Franklin; and I have no doubt he will persevere this time also. By the time you get this we shall be far off on the wide Atlantic. By the end of September you may expect to hear from me by the transport. Till then farewell, my dear Katie. My kindest love to Lewie.—Your affectionate brother,   JOHN IRVING.

Tuesday morning.—We are off Stromness now, and I send this on shore by the Orkney pilot, who is about to leave us. The steamers accompany us a hundred miles further. Farewell for a couple of months more.

The following letter is the last. Whale-fish Island seems to correspond nearly with Upernavick, on the west coast of Greenland, the most northerly of the Danish settlements in that country.

H.M.S. "TERROR,"
WHALEFISH ISLAND, GREENLAND,
Probably 10*th July* 1845.

MY DEAR KATE,—I sit down at last to take a long farewell of you, for it will be probably a couple of years, if not more, before I have another opportunity to write. I wrote you from Orkney, where we stopped three days. We left there on the 2d of June, and had a voyage of a month, with the usual variety of fair and foul weather. We made the coast of Greenland on the 25th, and arrived at the Whale-fish Islands on the 4th instant. We have been very busy shifting our stores and provisions from the transport, which has convoyed us so far. We have now cleared her of everything, and we all sail to-

morrow,—she on her voyage back to England, and
we, in the first place, for Barrow's Strait, and after,
as we best can. Only three of the cattle on board
the transport have survived the voyage; however,
we leave this with three complete years' provisions,
so, even should we not cast up for so long, you need
not think we have been eating our shoes. About
the last week of September we shall fix our ships
somewhere for the winter. We shall be frozen up
for ten months, several of which in total darkness.
At present we have constant daylight, and for the
last fortnight we have had sunshine all night.
There is plenty of ice floating about and scraping
our sides, and we have sometimes a little snow.
All very well for July.

I have every cause to be pleased with my shipmates, and barring the want of all communication,
I ought to enjoy myself very much, as everything is
new, and, after all, there is nothing like variety—at
least it is so at sea.

The Whalefish Islands, where we now are, consist
of four or five barren rocky islands like Inchkeith,
and the openings betwixt some of the islands are
choked up with ice. We have passed many icebergs,
which are huge piles of ice and snow floating about.
Some are 200 feet high. These are formed by

avalanches from the Greenland mountains, which
are very high and precipitous, and one sheet of snow
to the water's edge.   There are some families of
Esquimaux living here—most wretched people, half-
starved, living on seals (when they can catch them);
but they seem happy, and they can read their own
language, and have Bibles sent from Denmark,
printed in Esquimaux, and they have been taught
to read by a Danish missionary who was here some
years ago. They are dressed in sealskin jackets, etc.,
women and all alike, and their children, of which
there are great numbers, are very curious-looking
creatures, more like seals than anything else.   They
have rosy cheeks, and round, good-humoured faces
though rather greasy.   Their canoes are just long
enough to sit in, and the sealskin frock is tied round
the edge of the hole they sit in, to keep the water

out; so they can go right under water without taking
any in. They are made of sealskins covering a frame

made of bones, and are so light that a man can carry them.   You will see all these things far better described in the Polar voyages of Parry, Ross, and Back, which perhaps you may now have a little interest in looking at, as they describe exactly what will be our difficulties ; and you will, I daresay, like to know a little what I may be about for so long ; at least, I am sure you have no friend that takes a greater interest in you than I do.   I send you a little Polar chart, and I have put the track of the Expedition in red, and proposed route dotted red.   We hope to reach Melville Island before the end of September, and pass the winter there, and try to reach Behring's Straits the following summer.

Should the ice not clear away enough, or should we meet land instead of water, we shall have to pass another winter and try again, and either to go on or come back in the third summer.

The former Expeditions were stopped by a barrier of ice so thick and solid that the summer, which is only ten weeks long, passed away without dissolving it.   However, I trust we may have a warmer summer, either this or the next, or find some channel which they overlooked.   We have the advantage of all their experience, and will save much valuable time in not looking uselessly for a passage where

land has been laid down in their charts, which we
have with us. We have a library of the best books
of all kinds, consisting of 1200 volumes, and shall
be able to pass the time very well, as there shall be
some exploring parties sent out on foot while the
ships are frozen in ; and we will eke out our provisions with all the game our guns can procure.
We shall be very busy sawing the ice and working
the ships on, whenever a single mile can be gained.
I have written my father a letter which is very
much to the same effect as this. You might send
him the little chart, as our proposed route is shown
in it, and he is much interested in geography generally; I daresay you may see my letter to him.
And now you are in possession of all I can tell
you.

The sudden change from summer back to winter
has caused us all to suffer from chilblains. Some
are so bad that they cannot put on their shoes.
I have had my hands much swollen ; but they
say that in two or three weeks all this will go
away. There are many tons of ice within five
or six yards of me now ; but it is not cold, and the
sun shining all night, we don't think of going to
bed, but go shooting after working hours are over,
and it is supposed to be night. We shall have

it dark for a long time by and by. I must now finish, my dear Katie. May every good attend you and yours. My kindest love to my dear father and Lewis.—Yours ever affectionately,

JOHN IRVING.

P.S.—I have been making sketches; but you will see all of them when I next come to Falkirk. I have eight hours' watch out of the twenty-four to keep on deck, and I have charge of our chronometers, which are little clocks. I have to wind them up and compare them, and write an account of their goings on—there are ten of them in each ship,—and also various astronomical observations to make, and calculations. All this is much more interesting than the dull routine in a regular man-of-war, which is like a barrack or a workhouse. Now, good-bye. God bless you.

We are going to have a school for the men. Our Captain reads prayers on Sundays. We are exempt from many of the temptations of the world, and I hope we shall have grace to find that it has been good for us to have been separated from the world, and that God has been with us in all our wanderings. May we submit ourselves to His pleasure in all things.

I send you a small piece of the *Tripe de Roche*, a sort of lichen growing on the rocks, which was the food of Sir John Franklin in his Expedition. I send you a sketch of our ships at this place. The "Erebus" is alongside of the transport getting her provisions, and the "Terror" is a little to the left. The Danish house is in front, and two Esquimaux sealskin tents, which they live in during summer.

"EREBUS" and "TERROR" at Whalefish Island, July 1845. Storeship alongside, transferring provisions to one of the ships. From a sketch by Lieutenant Irving, enclosed in his last letter. P. 122.

CHAPTER VII.

HERE the curtain falls, so to speak, and John Irving and all his healthy and hopeful comrades pass out of view, and become virtually silent to their friends and countrymen. The "Erebus" and "Terror" were seen by a single passing whaler after leaving the Whalefish Islands; but after that nothing was seen or heard of them by the civilised world for many long years. They disappeared amid the frost and snow and long winter darkness of the Arctic regions.

Many experienced navigators hoped almost against hope that they, or at least a remnant of the Expedition, might yet appear, for they knew and believed in the experience, the resources, and persistent courage of the man who led the enterprise, and they were

confident that all that could be done would
be done by adventurous courage under the
circumstances. But years passed by without any tidings, and then fresh Expeditions
were fitted out, not so much for discovering
the desiderated North-West Passage by Behring's Straits, as for ascertaining the fate of Sir
John Franklin and his gallant crews, and of
helping them if still within the reach of human
aid. These Expeditions, although carefully
planned, and carefully carried out with all the
bravery and patience so characteristic of our
naval service, were uniformly unsuccessful as
to the primary object; but great additions
were made by all of them towards an accurate
knowledge of the Arctic archipelago. It is
very interesting and instructive to compare
the sketch map of the Arctic regions at the
time of Franklin's last voyage, as given by
Sir Leopold M'Clintock in his narrative,
with maps of the same region at the present
time. It would seem, that when the long-
sought North-West Passage was beginning

to lose its attractive power after repeated
failure and disappointment, a new stimulus
was found to geographical exploration and discovery in the great solicitude felt for Franklin
and his brave companions. Doubtless the
God of Providence and of Grace has jewels
for the Redeemer's crown even in these in-
hospitable regions, and they must be brought
within hearing of the Gospel through human
enterprise and energy. It would be incon-
sistent with the purpose and scope of this
small volume, even were we able, to enter
into any detailed account of the accurate
and valuable contributions which have been
made since 1845, when Sir John Franklin
commenced his voyage, by such men as
James Ross, Collinson, Maclure, Belcher,
Osborn, Browne, Rae, Anderson, M'Clintock,
Hobson, and Young. Their works are acces-
sible to all who take a special interest in
such matters, and will amply repay a careful
perusal. Notwithstanding these accessions
to our knowledge of the geography of these

sterile regions, little valuable light was
thrown on the fate of Franklin and his
companions until Sir Leopold M'Clintock
published his "Voyage of the Fox." Rae,
when exploring a part of the Boothia Isthmus
in 1854, heard from certain Esquimaux, that
some years before, during spring, a party of
about forty white men had been seen travelling over the ice, and dragging a boat along
the coast of King William Land. It was
added, that later in the season of the same
year, the bodies of about thirty men were
found on the continent and five on an island
near the mouth of the Great Fish River. At
the same time some relics, believed to be of
the Franklin Expedition, were bought from
the natives and sent home. These are deposited and preserved in the Naval and
Military Museum, London. This information gave an encouraging clew to further
inquiry, and led to the Fox Expedition
under Captain M'Clintock, who, at the
urgent request of Lady Franklin, gener-

ously undertook the heroic task of making a new search for her husband and his gallant company. He did his work in the most thorough manner, and, after difficulties and perils of a very remarkable kind, succeeded in clearing up the long-hidden story of the Franklin Expedition.

During April and May 1859, Captain M'Clintock and Lieutenant Hobson, travelling from their winter quarters in sledges drawn by dogs, examined part of the west coast of Boothia, the whole of the shores of King William Island, the mouth of the Great Fish River, and Montreal Island. M'Clintock also collected information, with great diligence, from the Esquimaux whom he met at various points. The main result of his search, however, was the discovery of a record at Cape Victory, near the north-western corner of King William Land. This record, written between the lines and round the available margin of one of the printed forms usually supplied to discovery ships, contains all the reliable information which we have either about *itself* or about the history of Sir John Franklin's Expedition. It was written at two different times. The first portion by Lieutenant Graham Gore, who with Charles des Vœux, mate, and six men, had left the ship four days previously, intending probably, as M'Clintock suggests, to examine the unknown line of coast of King William Land, betwixt Point Victory and Cape Herschel. It bore date May 28th, 1847. This portion, as we learn from the second portion, had been deposited by Gore and his men, in June 1847, under a cairn supposed to have been built by Sir James Ross in 1831. It had been found in the following spring by our friend Lieutenant John Irving, and the second portion having been added by another hand, the completed document was transferred to a place four miles further south, which they had come to regard as the *true* position of Sir James Ross's pillar ; and there, in that solitude, the document thus written in instalments, so to speak,

H M. S. ships Erebus and Terror

28 of May 1847 { Wintered in the Ice in
{ Lat. 70° 5' N Long. 98° 23' W

Having wintered in 1846—7 at Beechey Island
in Lat 74° 43' 28" N. Long 91° 39' 15" W after having
ascended Wellington Channel to Lat 77° and returned
by the West side of Cornwallis Island

Commander.

Sir John Franklin commanding the Expedition

all well

WHOEVER finds this paper is requested to forward it to the Secretary of
the Admiralty, London, *with a note of the time and place at which it was
found*: or, if more convenient, to deliver it for that purpose to the British
Consul at the nearest Port.

QUINCONQUE trouvera ce papier est prié d y marquer le tems et lieu ou
il l'aura trouvé, et de le faire parvenir au plutot au Secretaire de l'Amirauté
Britannique à Londres.

CUALQUIERA que hallare este Papel, se le suplica de enviarlo al Secretario
del Almirantazgo, en Londrés, con una nota del tiempo y del lugar en
donde se halló.

EEN ieder die dit Papier mogt vinden, wordt hiermede verzogt, om het
zelve, ten spoedigste, te willen zenden aan den Heer Minister van de
Marine der Nederlanden in s Gravenhage, of wel aan den Secretaris der
Britsche Admiraliteit, in London, en daar by te voegen eene Nota,
inhoudende de tyd en de plaats alwaar dit Papier is gevonden geworden.

FINDEREN af dette Papiir ombedes, naar Leilighed gives, at sende
samme til Admiralitets Secretairen i London, eller nærmeste Embedsmand
i Danmark, Norge, eller Sverrig. Tiden og Stædit hvor dette er fundet
önskes venskabeligt paategnet.

WER diesen Zettel findet, wird hier durch ersucht denselben an den
Secretair des Admiralitets in London einzusenden, mit gefälliger angabe
an welchen ort und zu welcher zeit er gefundet worden ist.

Party consisting of 2 officers and 6 men
left the Ships on Monday 24th May 1847

remained until discovered by Sir Leopold
M'Clintock and his comrades in 1859.

With this explanation, we are able to
understand what had happened.

After passing through Lancaster Sound as
far as Barrow's Strait, they ascended Wellington Channel to lat. 77°, 150 miles, and,
returning by the west side of Cornwallis
Island, wintered at Beechy Island in 1845-6.
In the summer of 1846 they sailed to the
south-west, and reached within twelve miles
of the north extreme of King William Land,
where their further progress was arrested by
the approaching winter of 1846-7. They had
already made real discoveries, for the mere
entrance to Wellington Sound had been discovered by Parry; they had ascended it
and returned to Barrow's Strait by Queen
Channel, adding to our charts the extensive
lands on either side. Thus arrested and
beset in the ice, they passed the winter of
1846-7 in lat. 70° 5′ N., long. 98° 23′ W.

On the 24th of May 1847, as already mentioned, the party under Gore started on their

exploring route along the coast of King William Land. On the 28th the first part of the record was written, and in June it was deposited where Irving found it many months afterwards. It mentioned that Sir John Franklin was still in command, and ended with a cheerful *All well.*

A second winter in the ice followed— 1847-8,—and before another summer came, a melancholy change of circumstances had taken place. Another hand, probably that of Fitz-James, now Captain of the " Erebus," wrote as follows on the paper which Gore had deposited and Irving had found :—

April 25*th,* 1848.—H.M.S. "Terror" and "Erebus" were deserted on the 22d April, 5 leagues N.N.W. of this, having been beset since 12th September 1846. The officers and crews, consisting of 105 souls, under the command of Captain F. R. M. Crozier, landed here, in latitude 69° 37′ 42″, long. 98° 41′ W., and start to-morrow, the 26th, for Back's Fish River. Sir John Franklin died on the 11th of June 1847, and the total loss by death in the Expedition has been to this date, 9 officers and 15 men.

This was signed by Captain Crozier of the " Terror " and Captain Fitz-James of the " Erebus."

No mention is made of the return of Graham Gore and his exploring party ; but the second portion of the record speaks of him as the *late* Commander Gore, so that he probably died during the winter of 1847-8, which proved fatal to so many.

A facsimile of this record, so full of interest and so touching, seems worthy of being preserved in this memoir of one who had a good deal to do with it.

We refer our readers to M'Clintock's interesting narrative for other details which will assist them to realise more fully the probable history of the Expedition.   But the record, the contents of which have been already explained, affords all the exact and reliable information that we possess or can now look for.   Mr. C. R. Markham, C.B., Secretary of the Royal Geographical Society, in the Proceedings for November 1880, while giving an account of the recent expedition of

Lieutenant Schwatka, confirms this remark
so forcibly that we have much pleasure in
quoting what he says :—

There is nothing else but conjecture, based on
the vague and unreliable stories of the Esquimaux,
and inference derived from relics and their positions.
With these as a means of illustrating the facts of
the record, M'Clintock pieced together the sad but
heroic story. The ground at Cape Victory was
strewn with great quantities of clothes and stores,
pointing to the probability that the survivors had
overrated their strength, and were obliged to lighten
the boats which they were dragging on heavy sledges.
The discovery of Lieutenant Hornby's sextant made
it probable that he was among those who landed.
Farther on, in Erebus Bay, one of the boats was
found on a sledge, with two bodies in it, and many
relics of various kinds. Among them was a Bible,
The Vicar of Wakefield, and a little volume of
private devotions which Sir George Back had presented to his old friend, Graham Gore. Perhaps it
was the thoughtful act of some messmate to bring
away the little book for the relations of the deceased
officer. The boat's head was pointed back to the
ships, indicating that a portion of the retreating

crews had broken down, and that an attempt was made to return to the ships and bring back fresh supplies of food. The rest pushed on, and M'Clintock found a skeleton beyond Cape Herschel, proving that *they discovered the North-West Passage.* But the great majority of the bodies probably fell through the ice on which they walked, when the thaw came, and found a last resting-place in the great deep. The information carefully collected from Esquimaux by Mr. Petersen, M'Clintock's interpreter, was to the effect that many of the white men dropped by the way as they went to the Great Fish River; that some were buried, and some were not, a fact discovered by the Esquimaux during the following winter, and corroborated by the position of the skeleton which M'Clintock found beyond Cape Herschel. It was also ascertained that one ship had been seen to sink in deep water, and that the other was forced on shore by the ice. On board the latter the body of a tall man was found, but there was little then left of the wreck, the position of which was indicated. At one time the natives had seen many books and papers, but they had all been thrown away or destroyed long before. It was clear that the record at Cape Victory would furnish the only certain intelligence we should ever receive.

While this is substantially the case, Captain Hall and Lieutenant Schwatka of America, with commendable zeal and good feeling, have succeeded, after much personal exertion, in adding some illustrative details to the sad story of the Franklin Expedition.

Captain Hall [says Mr. Markham], in May 1869 just touched the line of retreat at Todd's Island and Peffer River. He heard that seven bodies were buried at these places, and he brought home bones supposed to have been those of Lieutenant Le Vescomte of H.M.S. "Erebus." He heard the story of the wreck of the ship and the body of a tall man having been found on board, and he was also told that a boat and tent full of bodies were seen by the Esquimaux in Terror Bay, some miles south of the position in which M'Clintock and Hobson found the boat. There is nothing improbable in the latter story, but it is not corroborated by Lieutenant Schwatka, who carefully searched the spot. This, however, does not disprove it, as all traces might easily have been obliterated in the long lapse of time. Captain Hall also heard that the boat with the last survivors did not reach Montreal Island, but an inlet on the west side of the promontory which terminates at Point Richardson. Lieutenant Schwatka (ten years later) confirms the accuracy of Hall's information on this last point. The natives told him that a boat and a number of skeletons were seen near the water-line in this inlet, and that books and papers were scattered among the rocks and long since lost. The boat was turned over and the skeletons beneath it. One body, perhaps that of the last survivor (not an officer) was found five miles inland. An old woman also told Lieutenant Schwatka that she saw the retreating party dragging a sledge with a boat on it, and she described the personal appearance of three of the officers. One seems to have been a doctor. She also alleged that she saw the tent and dead bodies of which Hall heard at the head of Terror Bay.

Lieutenant Schwatka's personal search along the west coast of King William Island was not rewarded by any important discovery. The work of M'Clintock and Hobson had been done too thoroughly. Two of his companions, however, found the grave of an officer near Cape Victory. It was that of Lieutenant Irving of H.M.S. "Terror," as a silver medal was picked up close to it which proved to be a mathematical prize won by that officer at the Royal Naval College in 1830. The grave of another officer was

found near Point le Vescomte, and some bones of
five other different individuals. They were collected
and buried. Near Cape Felix two cairns were met
with, probably erected for taking bearings by parties
which landed during the year before the ships were
abandoned.

We already know enough. We knew that our
gallant countrymen died in discovering the North-
West Passage, and that they fell in the performance
of their duty. In Sherard Osborn's charming
memoir, and in the admirable narrative of Sir
Leopold M'Clintock, the heroic story of the fate of
Franklin will be read with unfailing interest by
generation after generation. And Englishmen will,
at the same time, always cherish a feeling of gratitude
for the kindly deed of the brave Americans who
tenderly collected and buried some of the bones of
our heroes, *and brought away the remains of one of
them,* a task which we well know entailed no small
amount of peril and hardship.

The relatives and friends of John Irving,
in compliance with whose desire this small
volume has been compiled, enter warmly into
these sentiments, so eloquently expressed by

Mr. Markham; and they will have much pleasure in seeing introduced at this place part of the narrative which he has recorded in the Proceedings of the Royal Geographical Society, of the Expedition of Lieutenant Schwatka to King William Land. The plan of the Expedition was novel. The scenes were new; and although the results did not add much to our knowledge of Sir John Franklin's fate, it seems both natural and fitting that the procedure by which they were attained should find a place in this memorial of one of his officers.

The party consisted of four white men, namely, Lieutenant Schwatka, Colonel W. H. Gilder (the author of the narrative), Henry Klutschek, and Frank Milnes. They wintered at Camp Daly, near the entrance of Chesterfield Inlet, on the west shore of Hudson's Bay, adapting themselves to the mode of life of the Esquimaux (or *Inuit*, as Colonel Gilder more correctly calls them), and making preliminary reconnoitring journeys.

It was Lieutenant Schwatka's intention to effect his purpose with the aid of natives and their dogs,

K

and his plan was to march across the unknown land between Chesterfield Inlet and the estuary of the Back River, and thence to examine the western side of King William Island—a formidable enterprise, which would certainly occupy many months.

The expedition left Camp Daly on the 1st of April 1879, with three sledges and a load of 5000 lbs. drawn by forty-two dogs. Besides walrus meat, the provisions consisted of biscuit, corn-starch, pork, compressed corned beef, cheese, tea, and molasses. But these supplies were not calculated to last more than a fraction of the time, being one month's provisions for the whole party. The main reliance was upon the game afforded by the region to be traversed. The party was entirely deprived of vegetable food; they took no lime-juice, and there was no scurvy; which is one more stubborn fact for the English Scurvy Committee. Besides the four white men, the party consisted of Joe the Esquimaux interpreter, and his wife; a splendid hunter and dog-driver named Too-loo-ah, and his wife and child; two other *Inuit* men, with their wives and a child each, and two lads: altogether thirteen *Inuit* men, women, and children.

During the months of April and May the party marched across a high country of rolling hills, with much snow and occasional deep drifts. The thermometer was above freezing, and the sun insufferably hot. Plenty of reindeer were seen nearly every day, the herds being often chased by wolves, which also prowled round the camp. The game indeed was so abundant, that besides bears, and seals, and four musk-oxen, the party obtained during the journeys out and home no less than 522 reindeer.

The landscape, though sombre and forbidding, was grand, and occasionally presented scenes of great beauty. In the first week of May they crossed the Arctic Circle, and soon afterwards came upon a branch of the Back River, which they followed for ninety miles. It flows through a gorge with dark hills rising to 800 or 1000 feet on either side. On the 22d of May they reached the estuary of the Back River, having travelled all the way through a country filled with game, and having seen two or three large herds of reindeer every day. The river, which led them to the Back estuary, was named after the President of the United States.

Lieutenant Schwatka visited Montreal Island, and then crossed the land to an inlet west of Richardson Point, collecting many stories from the Esquimaux. In June he crossed over to Cape Herschel, on King William Island, and examined

the western shore, with the greatest care, for relics
of the Franklin Expedition, as far as Cape Felix,
the northern extremity of the island.

We have already mentioned the results of
this Expedition, in which much labour was
put forth, and innumerable difficulties and
inconveniences encountered.

The achievement of Lieutenant Schwatka and his
companions is most remarkable, and in some respects
his journey is without a parallel.   It reflects the
highest credit on the commander and on those who
served under him so admirably ; and it is certain
the work could not have been done without natural
qualities of a very high order, combined with careful
training and the most thoughtful adaptation of the
best attainable means to the end in view.   The
English nation, and more especially its naval service
and its geographers, have received the news of this
noble effort to obtain more complete intelligence of
our lost heroes with feelings of warm gratitude to
Lieutenant Schwatka and his gallant companions, as
well as to those who generously supplied the means
and gave the instructions under which the explorers
acted.

CHAPTER VIII.

WE have quoted largely from Mr. Markham's paper; and we are further indebted to him for some accurate statements in regard to the professional life of John Irving, and also for a lucid commentary, the result of much thought and consideration upon the *probable* course of events after the "Erebus" and "Terror" disappeared within the Arctic Circle. We make no apology for culling some of these from an interesting document which Mr. Markham has taken the trouble of preparing in illustration of the subject so unexpectedly opened up afresh by the discovery of Irving's remains.

As we know from his letters, Irving joined

the " Excellent " with the view of qualifying
himself more thoroughly in gunnery and other
professional subjects, and was appointed third
lieutenant of H.M.S. " Terror " on the 13th
of March 1845. The following is a list of
the officers who sailed in that ship :—

> Captain Crozier.
> Lieutenants Little, Hodgson, Irving.
> Mates Hornby and Thomas.

Irving [says Mr. Markham] was a talented drafts-
man. He had an iron constitution, and was well
adapted for Arctic service.[1]

I incline to the belief that Little and Hodgson
died during the winter of 1847-8. Hodgson was in
bad health when he left England with a delicate
chest.

When the retreating crews landed in April 1848,
Crozier was in command, with Irving as his second.

---

[1] An Orkney lady, who still survives, and remembers being
introduced to and shaking hands with him in the cabin of the
" Terror " while in Stromness harbour, writes :—" Lieutenant
Irving was very conspicuous among the officers who were that
day in the cabin of the ' Terror,' by his greater appearance of
manly strength and calm decision—one apparently well fitted
for the hardships foreseen but not dreaded. A general feeling
of sure success pervaded them all."

Fitz-James was in command of the "Erebus," with Le Vescomte as his second (Graham Gore having died in the winter).

Irving is mentioned in the record found by M'Clintock at Point Victory, as having discovered the record deposited in the previous year (1847) by Graham Gore and Des Vœux, at a point four miles north of Point Victory. This proves that Irving was still active and comparatively well when they landed on April 25th (record says the 22d).

The whole party set out for the Fish River on April 26th. Information received from the natives by Hall and Schwatka shows that a very large tent full of dead bodies, with graves near it, was found on the shore of Terror Bay. From this I conclude that about half of the whole number broke down at Terror Bay, unable to go further.

It would be the duty of *one* of the leaders to remain with the disabled, of the *other* to push on for help. It is clear that Crozier pushed on towards the Fish River, because the natives called the officer they met by the same name that Crozier had among them during Parry's second voyage. He no doubt reminded them of it. Fitz-James therefore remained at Terror Bay. His second, Le Vescomte, pushed on with those of the " Erebus " who were still able to walk, for Hall found his skeleton on Todd Island. As Crozier went on, his second, Irving, would have remained with the disabled men of the "Terror."

So we have Fitz-James and Irving remaining with the sick at Terror Bay, aided by a few able-bodied volunteers, probably officers. These heroic men had then to decide what next to do. The sick would soon need more provisions and medical comforts. It would be necessary to return to the ships and bring back all that was left there. Fitz-James would probably remain with the sick and disabled, sharing their misery and privations; Irving would command the returning party. The large boat was dragged back to Erebus Bay, but there their strength failed them. A few who had broken down were left there with provisions; the rest, under Irving, pushed shipwards. The gallant hero had taxed his strength to the uttermost. He fell gloriously at Point Victory, where stones were piled over his body by his dying comrades. The Royal Naval College medal was buried with him, and found by Schwatka. This is what I believe to have happened, after giving the subject much thought.

The officers distributed their plate (spoons and forks) among the men when the ships were abandoned. But none of Irving's plate was found,—

only the medal. The total number of pieces of plate found was sixty-four.

The North-West Passage was discovered when Cape Herschel was reached. This was probably accomplished by the travelling party under Graham Gore and Des Vœux in June 1847. If not then, by Crozier and Le Vescomte, and the party that pushed on to the mouth of the Fish River in May 1848.

The record, April 1848, says that nine officers had died. Sir John Franklin and Graham Gore are stated in the record to have died. The two ice-masters, Blanbury and Reid, and the parson Osmer, were old men, and probably died in the winter. Little and Hodgson, lieutenants of the "Terror," had, I think, died. Young Des Vœux was, I think, dead, because Irving is mentioned as having discovered the record deposited by Graham Gore and Des Vœux the year before. If Des Vœux had landed there would have been no need to search for it. Helpman, the clerk, was, I think, the ninth officer that had died. Therefore, fifteen officers landed at Point Victory on the 25th of April 1848. These were :—

Terror.	*Erebus.*
Crozier.	Fitz-James.
Irving.	Le Vescomte.

Terror.	Erebus.
Hornby.	Fairholme.
Thomas.	Sargent.
Macbean.	Conch.
Dr. Peddie.	Dr. Stanley.
Dr. Macdonald.	Dr. Goodsir.
	Collins.

Party that pushed on to the Fish River:—
Crozier.
Le Vescomte (died at Todd Island).
Fairholme.
Dr. Stanley (stick found at Montreal Island).
Hornby.

Party that remained with sick at Terror Bay:—
Fitz-James.
* Irving.
Sargent.
Thomas.
* Conch (died in the boat).
Macbean.
Collins.
Dr. Peddie.
* Dr. Macdonald.

* Officers returning to the ships for more supplies.

We add the following summary of dates, also supplied by Mr. Markham:—

1845. *May* 19. The Franklin Expedition left the Thames, provisioned for three years.

1845. *July*   4. Arrived at Whalefish Island.

,,   ,, 26. Last seen in Baffin's Bay by a whaler.

,,   *August.* Sailed up Wellington Channel to 77° N.

1845-6. Wintered at Beechy Island.

1846. *Jany.* 1. J. Tovington of H.M.S. "Terror" died, aged twenty.

,,   ,,   4. J. Hortwell, A.B. "Erebus," died, aged twenty-five.

,,   *April* 3. Wm. Braine, marine of "Erebus," died, aged thirty-two.

(Ascertained from the three graves in Beechy Island.)

,,   *Sept.* 12. Beset in 70° 5' N. and 98° 28' W.

1846-7. Wintered in the Pack.

1847. *May* 28. Graham Gore and Des Vœux and party left the ships. *All well.*

,,   *June* 11. Sir John Franklin died.

1847-8. Wintered in the Pack. Twenty-one, nine officers and twelve men, died.

1848. *April* 22. Ships abandoned five leagues N.N.W. of Point Victory. 105 souls landed.

,,   25. Record signed at Point Victory by Crozier, Fitz-James.

1848. *April* 26. Start for Back's Fish River.

1859. Their fate discovered by M'Clintock.

1879. Irving's medal and his remains recovered
and brought away by Schwatka.

The short but eventful career which we
have been contemplating suggests more
than one topic for pensive thought. That
John Irving was fashioned by successive
stages of his experience for his ultimate
occupation as an Arctic explorer, must be
manifest. His successful training in mathematics, his love for boating and general seamanship, his turn for natural philosophy,
his adventurous ascent of Etna under excep-
tional difficulties, his expertness in rescuing
in two instances companions from a watery
grave, his solitary life of hardness in the
bush during four years, his subsequent
familiarity with exploring service in the
South seas, were all fitted to prepare him
for the duties which awaited him in the
Franklin Expedition. What was the issue
of it all ? No doubt, as we have seen, that

unfortunate company of devoted men really
made some additions to the geography of
the Arctic regions ; but, humanly speaking,
the Expedition, with no fault of theirs, was
a comparative failure in a scientific point
of· view. This admission, however, leads us
to observe, that in other respects, moral and
religious, it may turn out eventually to have
been a great success.   There is surely something noteworthy, and even remarkable, in
the circumstance by which a fresh interest
has been unexpectedly awakened in an
enterprise which had been almost forgotten
after the lapse of so many long years—
years filled with a constant succession of
exciting events daily becoming historical.
A silver medal conferred on a mere boy,
half a century before, which used to lie on his
fond father's business-table in Edinburgh, is
picked up covered with the grime of a grave
which had been rifled by greedy natives of
King William Land in quest of plunder.
It had rested there for thirty-one years,

and had escaped notice until picked up by
the adventurous Americans who had undertaken the self-imposed task of throwing still
further light on the course of our naval
heroes whom M'Clintock had already tracked
so far.

This medal led, we think very reasonably,
to the identification of the remains, and
created a new interest in many who had
ceased to think of the whole affair in any
other light than as a melancholy episode
in our naval history. A public funeral
followed with imposing formalities. This
led to a not unnatural curiosity in regard
to the individual, hitherto little known, who
had suddenly and unexpectedly become the
representative of a whole company of heroic
men, whose memory their country had pleasure in honouring. Forthwith a number of
private letters came to light, which friendship had carefully treasured all these years,
although to have destroyed them would,
perhaps, have been a more likely course

of procedure. When it turns out that
these letters, besides illustrating an eventful
life, show also that the writer was a man of
strong religious convictions and deep earnest-
ness, we begin to surmise that the All-wise
and overruling God of Providence may
have had a great purpose in the foregoing
chain of circumstances. It is well known
that Sir John Franklin himself was a pro-
nounced Christian, and we have the testi-
mony of one contemporary at least, still
alive, to the fact, that several of his subor-
dinates, besides Lieutenant Irving, bore a
similar character,—all the necessary preparations for the exploring Expedition having
been gone about by them in a devotional
spirit very noticeable to their associates.
No one can tell what an important influence
these God-fearing men may have exercised
during these gloomy years of Arctic experience, both in sustaining the hearts of their
comrades amid the stupendous trials of their
lot, and in teaching them—mainly by their

consistent example—the *one* true way of facing the unseen world which lay before them.

Is it too much to indulge the hope that this simple memorial sketch of John Irving may, with the Divine blessing, be the means of leading other young men of heroic aspirations to consecrate their lives more completely to His service?

Our great poet has said truly—

"There's a Divinity that shapes our ends,
Rough-hew them how we will."

APPENDIX.

I.

From the *Edinburgh Daily Review* and other sources we give the following description of Lieutenant Irving's funeral :—

Edinburgh, 8th January 1881.—Yesterday the closing incident in the story of the ill-fated Franklin Expedition of 1845 was witnessed, when in this city the bones of a gallant member of that Expedition, which have for over thirty years been resting in an unknown grave, were re-interred by relatives grateful for the chance which had placed it within their power thus to perform the last kindly offices to one whom they had loved in life and mourned in death. That a vast concourse of people should have thronged the streets through which the funeral *cortége* was expected to pass was but natural, as it was well known that every honour which customarily attends the burial of an officer of her Majesty's service was to be given to the deceased, and the expectation of witnessing a spectacle imposing in character was sufficient to induce many to endeavour to gain a view of the procession in passing. But among the greater number of those

L

who lined the thoroughfares sight-seeing formed
no incentive to be present. The general feeling
seemed to be one of deep admiration for the memory
of the departed; of sympathy at the recollection of
the circumstances attending his death; and a sincere
desire to testify the interest and appreciation by an
intelligent public of an able, devoted, and worthy
officer and gentleman, to whom death came while in
the discharge of a noble duty. The funeral took
place from the house of Mrs. William Scott-
Moncrieff, the sister of Lieutenant Irving, where,
prior to the hour for starting, a number of relatives
and personal friends were assembled. These com-
prised Rev. John Irving, nephew; W. G. Scott-
Moncrieff, advocate, nephew; D. M. Peebles,
banker; R. C. Bell, W.S.; and T. S. Omond,
St. John's College, Oxford, nephews by marriage;
H. D. Hay, M.D.; Dr. R. B. Malcolm; J. H. W.
Rolland, C.A.; District Commissary-General A.
Clerk; Dr. Andrew Wood; Rev. A. Whyte; Rev.
Mr. Cowan of Troon; Messrs. J. Adam; W. E.
Malcolm of Burnfoot, in early life a messmate of
the deceased; J. Scott-Moncrieff, C.A.; Benjamin
Bell, F.R.C.S.; Stuart Neilson, W.S.; William Wood,
C.A.; Henry Cadell of Grange; H. J. Rollo, W.S.

A service having been conducted in the house by
the Rev. A. Whyte, the coffin, which was of polished
oak, and covered with the Union Jack, was carried
out by six seamen, and placed on a gun-carriage
from Leith Fort, drawn by six horses, and in charge
of a sergeant. The procession then moved off in
slow time, headed by a strong firing party of Marines

from the "Lord Warden" under Captain Sweny and
Lieutenant M'Causland, R. M. L. I. Then came the
band and pipers of the 71st Regiment and the gun-
carriage bearing the remains. These were followed
by Captain Lindesay Brine, R.N., and Major-General
Irving, R.A., C.B., as chief mourners. Then the
relatives and immediate friends. Next followed the
seamen of the "Lord Warden," as mourners, under
Captain Kingscote, R.N. The other naval officers
marched on each side of the gun-carriage, as pall-
bearers, and were—Lieutenants Johnson, Field,
Monteith, Reid, and Ede. After these came an
officer and twenty men each from the 21st Hussars,
the Royal Artillery, and the 71st H. L. I. In
the rear followed Major-General Hope, C.B., com-
manding the forces in Scotland, and the Head-
Quarter Staff, comprising Colonel Preston, A.A.G.,
Captain Salmond, D.A.A.G., and Captain Hope,
A.D.C., and then all the officers of the Edin-
burgh garrison off duty; Colonel Ingilby, R.A.;
Colonel Morrison, R.E.; Lieutenant-Colonel Jones,
R.A.; Lieutenant Blackman, R.A.; Major Locock,
R.E.; Lieutenant Conder, R.E.; Captains H. C.
Collier, A. P. Loyd, and W. W. Unett, Quarter-
master I. Kelly, and Lieutenant and Adjutant B.
Jennings, 21st Hussars; Major Allen, Captain F.
M. Reid, and H. A. Schank, Lieutenants E. W.
Horne, W. F. Anstey, J. Mitchell-Innes, Adjutant,
J. S. T. Farquhar, and I. C. Conway-Gordon; 71st
Regiment; and Major and Adjutant Hills, and
Captain Cranston, Q.E.R.V.B. There were present
Admirals Dunlop and Fellowes; Principal Sir A.

Grant, and other representatives of the University, members of the Town Council, Royal Society, and other public bodies. The Royal Geographical Society was represented by Captain Lindesay Brine, R.N.

A great crowd of people had assembled in Great King Street, and every minute its numbers were augmented.

From the lines formed by the Royal Navy and the troops the space to the railings in front of the houses was closely packed with spectators, while from the windows and balconies groups of ladies and children viewed the procession.

A start was made a few minutes before one o'clock, and the long line of márines, seamen, civilians, and officers marched between a double wall of human beings until the cemetery was reached.

The beautiful strains of the Maltese funeral hymn rose in the air, and to its slow and stately time the *cortége* moved on its progress westwards. The band was relieved at intervals by the melancholy plaint of " The Flowers of the Forest " from the bagpipes. The greatest order prevailed among the crowd, and the company proceeded in its slow march without interruption.

From Heriot Row the route was by Darnaway Street, the north division of Moray Place and Ainslie Place, and Great Stuart Street; and in all these streets every window and balcony was occupied, while the steps leading up to the houses were filled with people from the crowds in the streets who sought such vantage-ground to view the procession. The band were now playing Beethoven's funeral march, which in turn gave place to Handel's Dead March in Saul.

At the cemetery gate the firing party halted, opened out, faced inwards, and rested on their arms reversed. The coffin was taken from the gun-carriage, and, attended by the pall-bearers, was carried by six seamen to the grave, the procession passing into the cemetery through the double line of marines. The band followed, and the marines moved up and formed at the grave in readiness to fire the three farewell volleys.

The place of burial was towards the southern extremity of the cemetery, in close proximity to the tombs of Lords Jeffrey, Cockburn, Handyside, and Rutherfurd.

The service at the grave was conducted by the Rev. John Irving, after which the coffin,—which bore the inscription : " John Irving, Lieutenant R.N., born 1815 ; died 1848-1849 "—was lowered into the grave by Captain Lindesay Brine, Major-General Irving, and the pall-bearers, assisted by the six seamen who had carried the coffin from the gate to the grave.

Three volleys were then fired over the remains by the marines, the bugles of the 71st Regiment sounding after each volley. The various parties of the Royal Navy and military were then re-formed and moved off in quick time, and after a while were followed by the civilians, leaving to repose undisturbed those honoured bones so strangely discovered and conveyed so carefully to the brave Arctic voyager's native city.

II.

TESTIMONIALS in favour of the late Lieutenant J. IRVING, R.N., as to Good Conduct, Zeal, and Knowledge of his duty. Copied from Sir John Franklin's Papers left with Lady Franklin.

FROM ADMIRAL JAMES R. DACRES.

17th June 1843.

Mr. John Irving served as midshipman and mate on board H.M.S. "Edinburgh," under my command, from December 1833 to end of January 1837, during which period his conduct was that of an active, correct, and zealous officer, perfectly understanding his duty. I never had occasion to find fault with him during the whole of that period, and he joined me very strongly recommended by the Honourable Captain Dundas of H.M.S. "Belvidera."

JAS. R. DACRES,
Rear-Admiral.

FROM ADMIRAL SULIVAN.

These are to certify the Lords Commissioners of the Admiralty that Mr. John Irving served as mate on board H.M. sloop "Favourite" under my command from the 1st April 1842 to the date hereof, during which time he conducted himself with diligence, attention, and sobriety, and was always

obedient; and I further certify that he had charge
of a watch during the above period.

Given under my hand on board H.M. sloop
"Favourite," Hamoaze (Devonport Dock), this 20th
June 1843.   THOMAS R. SULIVAN,
                                   Commander.

FROM SIR WILLIAM DICKSON.

This is to certify that Lieutenant John Irving
has served on board H.M. ship "Volage" under my
command from the 30th of August 1843 to the date
hereof, during the whole of which period he com-
plied with the general printed instructions; and I
further certify that his conduct during the whole
time has merited my approbation, and I consider
him a steady and good officer.

Given under my hand on board H.M.S. "Volage,"
Cove of Cork, 31st December 1844.

                                   WM. DICKSON,
                                   Captain.

LIEUTENANT IRVING TO RIGHT HON. SIR G. CLERK.

                              H.M.S. "EXCELLENT,"
                              2d March 1845.

MY DEAR SIR GEORGE,—I am very desirous of
being appointed to one of the ships now fitting for
the Polar Expedition, and shall feel much obliged if
you can in any way forward my views.—Yours
truly,   JOHN IRVING.

Sir GEORGE CLERK, Bart.

RIGHT HON. SIR GEORGE CLERK, BART., TO ADMIRAL
SIR GEORGE COCKBURN.

BOARD OF TRADE, *3d March* 1845.

MY DEAR COCKBURN,—I herewith send you a
letter from my friend Lieutenant John Irving, now
serving on board the "Excellent," stating his desire
to be appointed to one of the ships now fitting for
the Polar Expedition.

As he possesses very considerable scientific attainments, I should consider him well qualified for a
service of this nature.

If all the appointments are not filled up, I should
be very much obliged to you to give him an appointment to one of the Polar Expedition vessels.—I
remain, yours truly,   G. CLERK.

The Right Honble.
Admiral Sir G. COCKBURN, G.C.B.

PRINTED BY T. AND A. CONSTABLE, PRINTERS TO HER MAJESTY,
AT THE EDINBURGH UNIVERSITY PRESS.

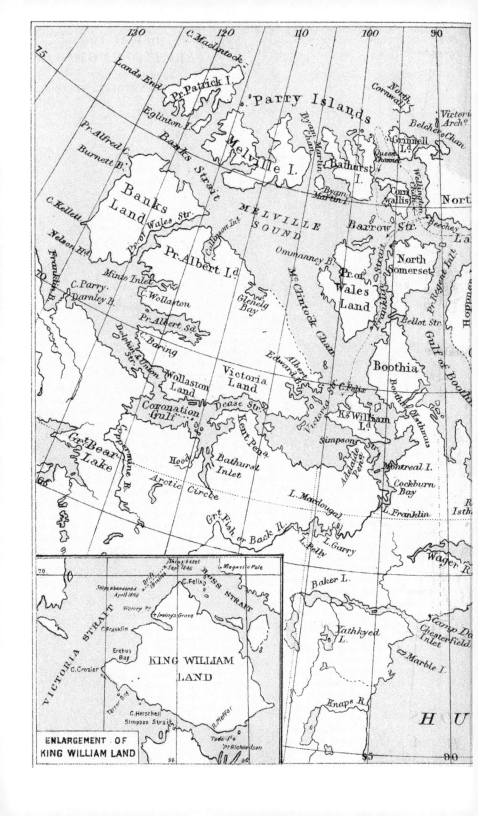

ENLARGEMENT OF
KING WILLIAM LAND

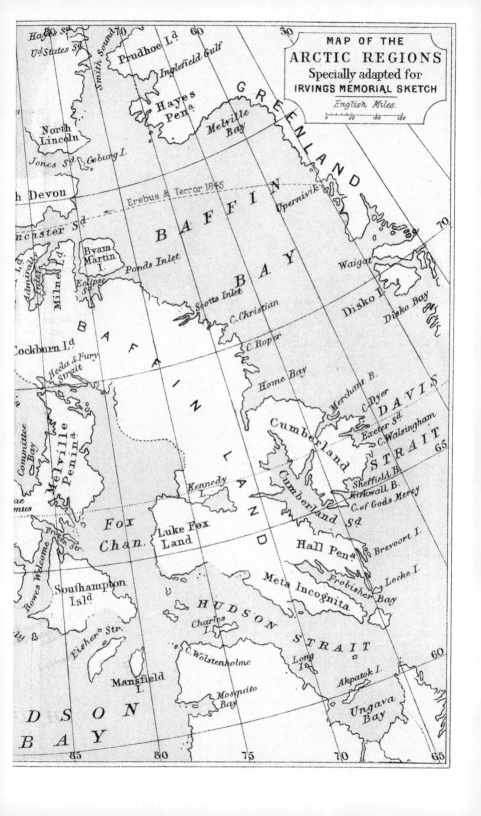

MAP OF THE
ARCTIC REGIONS
Specially adapted for
IRVINGS MEMORIAL SKETCH

English Miles.
0   50   100   150

For EU product safety concerns, contact us at Calle de José Abascal, 56–1°, 28003 Madrid, Spain or eugpsr@cambridge.org.

www.ingramcontent.com/pod-product-compliance
Ingram Content Group UK Ltd.
Pitfield, Milton Keynes, MK11 3LW, UK
UKHW012343130625
459647UK00009B/502